DISCIPLE IS A VERB

*Discovering Richness of Life
Through
Deeper Discipleship*

Robert McBurnett

TREATY OAK PUBLISHERS

PUBLISHER'S NOTE

Disciple is a Verb is a work of inspiration and individual memoir. All of the characters, business establishments, and events are based on the author's personal experiences. Individuals' names have been changed to protect their privacy. All quotes and references are shared by permission of each individual or owner. Scripture references unless otherwise noted are taken from the *World English Bible* (WEB) in the public domain. The name "World English Bible" is trademarked.

Copyright © 2016 by Robert McBurnett

Cover design by Kim Greyer
All rights reserved.

No part of this book may be reproduced, scanned, or distributed in any printed or electronic form without permission from the author. Please do not participate in or encourage piracy of copyrighted materials in violation of the author's rights. Purchase only authorized editions.

**Printed and published
in the United States of America**

TREATY OAK PUBLISHERS

ISBN-13: 978-1-943658-15-2
ISBN-10: 1-943658-15-3

DEDICATION

To my wife Christy,
the greatest gift a man ever received,
who is Jesus to me every day.
My love, my model, my ideal.

and

To my brothers and sisters of
Houston West Emmaus Community,
who led me to a fully committed walk
up Discipleship Road, for accompanying
me on the journey.

Praise for
DISCIPLE IS A VERB

Robert McBurnett gives us an everyman's answer to a simple question: how can I live and love like Jesus did? He cuts through theological mumbo jumbo and gives practical images and examples that both challenge and motivate. It is a great book for people who want to step out to do their faith rather than just go to church.

Tom Pace, Senior Pastor,
St. Luke's United Methodist Church, Houston

Disciple is a Verb is a call to all who profess Jesus as their Savior to put their faith into dynamic action. Robert McBurnett reminds us that our call to discipleship requires giving and receiving, and provides a straightforward framework for intentionally doing both. "Must read" is an over-used term for newly published books, and yet I cannot overstate the value of this book for any Christian seeking to grow in their personal relationship with Christ and to work more effectively for His Kingdom.

Steven R. Biegel, Executive Vice President,
Savills Studley

TABLE OF CONTENTS

INTRODUCTION	1
CHAPTER 1: Your Call to Discipleship	15
CHAPTER 2: What is a Disciple?	33
CHAPTER 3: What Does a Disciple Do?	55
CHAPTER 4: Being Discipled	85
CHAPTER 5: Discipling Others	121
CHAPTER 6: The Committed Disciple	155
CHAPTER 7: Discipleship Disciplines	169
CHAPTER 8: A Disciple For Life	195
CHAPTER 9: Growing in Discipleship	213
EPILOGUE: A Disciple in the World	241

DISCIPLE IS A VERB

*Discovering Richness of Life
Through
Deeper Discipleship*

Introduction

Yahweh of Armies says: "In those days, ten men will take hold, out of all the languages of the nations, they will take hold of the skirt of him who is a Jew, saying, 'We will go with you, for we have heard that God is with you.'"

Zechariah 8:23

"Our deepest fear is not that we are inadequate. Our deepest fear is that we are powerful beyond measure. It is our light, not our darkness, that most frightens us. We ask ourselves, 'Who am I to be brilliant, gorgeous, talented and fabulous?' Actually, who are you not to be? You are a child of God. Your playing small doesn't serve the world. There is nothing enlightened about shrinking so that others won't feel insecure around you. We were born to make manifest the glory of God that is within us. It's not just in some of us; it's in everyone. As we are liberated from our own fear, our presence automatically liberates others."

Nelson Mandela

So you want to be a disciple of Jesus Christ?

Great!

The inspiring strains of "I Have Decided to Follow Jesus"[1] well up inside you:

I have decided,

To follow Jesus.

No turning back.

Following Jesus is admirable, but you are called to discipleship. As a disciple you put Jesus center stage, no matter what phase of your faith walk you find yourself in at any given time. You want to set your faith on fire, transforming faith into an infectious, benevolent virus.

Look to Isaiah 40:28-31:

> *Haven't you known?*
> *Haven't you heard?*
> *The everlasting God, Yahweh,*
> *The Creator of the ends of the earth, doesn't faint.*
> *He isn't weary.*
> *His understanding is unsearchable.*
> *He gives power to the weak.*
> *He increases the strength of him who has no might.*
> *Even the youths faint and get weary,*
> *and the young men utterly fall;*
> *But those who wait for Yahweh will renew their*

strength.
They will mount up with wings like eagles.
They will run, and not be weary.
They will walk, and not faint.

We'll examine this passage in Chapter 1, but for now I want you to understand that true joy kicks in when we commit to walk with God. Walking with God... and not growing weary. Whether you are soaring, running, or walking, you can be on fire for the Lord. You can become his disciple rather than remaining a mere follower.

Becoming a disciple of Jesus Christ calls for much more than being a follower of Jesus Christ. It also requires your commitment to increasing in Christlikeness, and this book's objective is to intensify your discipleship. Our primary focus will be on growing in your personal discipleship and in reaching out to disciple others. Along the journey, we will explore God's call on your life, what a disciple is and does, and the disciplines and commitment required to sustain your growth as a disciple.

Being a follower is a quasi-passive endeavor. Becoming a disciple requires intentionality, commitment, and effort. Discipleship is not a spectator sport by any stretch of the imagination!

When you make your internal commitment to Christ, you take your first step toward following

Jesus. When you stand before a church congregation and make a public profession of faith, you have taken another significant step in following Jesus. When you make the intentional commitment to become more Christ-like in every aspect of your life, you have embarked on the road of a disciple.

Think of this distinction as analogous to the difference in reading and studying. Studying is much more purposeful and requires a higher degree of effort than merely reading, and so it is when you move from followership to discipleship.

For example, I keep up with several sports (primarily football) on multiple levels, and several of my friends yell for the same college football team I do. As casual followers, they hop on the Internet to see what our team is doing, and watch the games on TV.

In contrast, I invest in season tickets and attend all the home games, as well as travel from time to time to see our team play on the road. I too am a follower, a more committed follower, but a follower at best.

Travis, who sits next to me at home games, starts each morning on the Internet looking to see which players are excelling in practice and who is injured. He tracks the recruiting trail and can recite the career histories for each of our coaches. He is an amateur student of the game, but a student nonetheless.

In the sports vernacular, we're all fans, but Travis is a fanatic. To be a player or coach takes an even higher degree of commitment-an intentional, life course altering decision. These are the truly committed, dedicated, professional students of the game.

Here's another example. Suppose you track business and the stock market. You read the business pages every day, check the online market update sites, maybe you even subscribe to the Wall Street Journal. This level of commitment puts you in the follower category.

Suppose for a minute you quit your full-time job and become a day trader, which many people are tempted to do these days. By making that choice, you are relying on your ability to read the stock market accurately to provide your income. You have upped the ante. Your commitment elevates you to being a very interested student of the markets.

But when you elect a career as a financial advisor, your commitment level intensifies significantly, because in so doing you take responsibility for other people's money. You have to dedicate yourself to studying the markets and its underlying drivers. While you realize you will never fully master the twists and turns—the roller coaster nature—of the economy, you commit to learning and analyzing it on a daily basis. You have become a truly devoted, dedicated, professional student of the markets.

Now, let's apply this perspective to our relationship with God. God's design for our lives is to revert to our designed nature, which is to live in the presence of God. In the Garden of Eden, man and woman walked with God and shared his company (Genesis 1 and 2), but the relationship was broken when they collaborated to eat the fruit of the Tree of Knowledge of Good and Evil (Genesis 3). As a consequence of their disobedience, God cast out them of the Garden, but did not abandon them. Even in the act of banishing them, he provided clothing suitable for their journey (Genesis 3:21).

The remainder of the Bible chronicles God's repeated attempts to restore the original relationship in spite of our inability to uphold our end of the bargain. Our resistance and his persistence required him to go so far in his efforts to repair the relationship that he sent Jesus to walk among us, to implore us to follow him and to assure us he is the way to full restoration with God.

Jesus pleads for us to follow his example (John 1:43, 8:12, 10:27, and 12:26), and we grow in Christian discipleship as we grow in love for Jesus Christ,

Son of God. We do it by increasing our faith, which we cannot accomplish on our own. We must engage with others who guide us. My progress is the direct result of those who taught me along the way. Some walk just ahead and beckon to me like a loving parent, "Hurry up, let's go." Some walk beside me, setting the pace. Many others have gone before and call to me through personal memories or through their written words of guidance from which I learn and benefit.

The next step is to invite others we encounter along the way by nurturing them in their discipleship. Just as Jesus invites us into his kingdom, imploring us to take on the work of bringing the Kingdom, we must also invite others to share in the work.

The farther I venture down this Discipleship Road, the more apparent this two-pronged approach becomes. These are the two dimensions of discipleship we'll explore in depth in this book.

Our greatest fulfillment in this world comes in drawing close to God and in bringing others along with us. And it is Jesus who invites us in, first, by the invitation to follow him, and then the entreaty to bring others on the journey.

Similarly, the greatest legacy we can leave our children is unfinished business—worthy assignments we pass down—that commission them to advance God's mission. In a similar manner, we bless our followers when we articulate for them clear messages of the work yet to be done in bringing God's kingdom.

What confidence Jesus placed in his original twelve disciples, and in the generations of followers that would come along behind them... even to the end of the age! Not only does Jesus call us to follow him, but he also assures us we are no less than children of God.

We well remember his parting words to the disciples. *Go, and make disciples of all nations, baptizing them in the name of the Father and of the Son and of the Holy Spirit, teaching them to observe all things that I commanded you. Behold, I am with you always, even to the end of the age.* (Matthew 28:18-20). Herein lies the mission statement of his church: go and make disciples. Herein lies his steadfast assurance to his church: I am with you always, even to the end of the age.

In our efforts to render this charge manageable, we are tempted to simplify it by narrowing its scope. I often hear it interpreted as a call to spread God's word and make converts. Indeed, it does entail bringing the gospel to the world and introducing them to Jesus, but there is oh so much more to it than that.

When we limit our duty to spreading the word and bringing confessions for Christ, we have only accomplished a slice of what he is calling us to do. J. Oswald Sanders wrote, "It is significant that Jesus did not command his followers to go make believers or converts of all nations. His clear and unequivocal command was to go and make disciples. A disciple is simply a learner."[2]

I see far too many churches focusing all their efforts on this numbers game. "Look at all these confessions for Christ!" But once the newly converted are in the doors and on the rolls, these newborn Christians, brimming with the excitement of their new connection, are left to fend for themselves. Where is the assimilation? Where are the interconnections? Where are the personal relationships? Where is the personal growth? Where is the cultivation that leads to discipleship? Where is the closer walk with God?

Granted, it is the "church's" responsibility to follow-up with these new members, but when you get right to it, we are the church. This is not a laity/clergy matter. Certainly, the church administration can put structures in place to facilitate assimilation and engagement, but it is up to the laity to make it happen. Peter calls us into a holy and royal priesthood (1 Peter 2:5 and 9).

We are called by God to channel the energy and

unique perspectives of these new followers of Christ to reinvigorate our faith and passion. And they have so much to gain as they learn the joy of true humble servant-hood to the world around them; while we have just as much (or more) to learn from their fresh perspectives and budding exuberance. But these blessings will only come as we disciple them and in return continually grow as disciples.

Discipling is intentional.

Discipling takes effort.

Discipling is active.

Yes – disciple is a verb!

Disciple is not only a verb, but it is also an action verb. Bringing others along the path of discipleship is a conscious decision as we assume an active role in their spiritual growth. And we can only be effective in these efforts if we are simultaneously seeking to be coached by others, to be discipled in turn.

The words of Zechariah in 8:23 call out to me.

Yahweh of Armies says: "In those days, ten men will take hold, out of all the languages of the nations, they will take hold of the skirt of him who is a Jew, saying, 'We will go with you, for we have heard that

God is with you.' "

This passage speaks to grasping onto someone else, not just to follow them, but to become a committed disciple, dedicated to them and yearning to have what they have. This is not just an Old Testament concept either. It is most certainly rooted in the Old Testament, but we see it play out not only with Jesus and his disciples but carried forward in the relationship between Paul and Timothy, for example.

The first thing I want you to notice in this Zechariah passage is the Godly calling. This is God speaking—Yahweh of Armies, God, the Lord Almighty. These relationships exist because God ordained relationships in the natural order. God is calling his followers to introduce others to Christ, occasionally through teaching and conversation, but always through our actions and convictions.

As you spend time marinating in this passage, you will see it unfold in two layers. The first is fairly obvious: ten people have taken hold of the hem of the robe (skirt) of the Jew. There is little room for error here—they elect to follow this Jew—wherever he leads. They have discerned this Jew indeed walks with God and they want to be with this man. They are confident he will carry them into God's presence. More than mere followers, they have made the discipleship decision.

It is also an invitation to a journey, rather than an invitation to a location. These ten people do not join the Jew to be with him or even to study under him, but rather, they attach themselves tightly to him because of where he is going, "We will go with you!" Joining the Jew is not the end objective, instead going with him is their desire. They perceive he has not reached his destination and they want to GO with him.

I am dumbstruck when I contemplate Jesus summoning me to be with him; his invitation to engage in completing his work on earth completely overwhelms me. But it doesn't stop there. He has not left me to accomplish it on my own. Not only has he surrounded me with people to direct and encourage me in my disciple journey, but also he constantly places others in my path in the hope I will invite them to join in his work.

Which invokes the second dimension. At the same time I receive coaching along my faith walk, I am called to wear the robe of Christ and to disciple others. I am called to bring along those who seek to follow me as I follow him. This too is essential in the "making of disciples." This work is every bit as critical to bringing God's kingdom to fruition. We are to be intentional in our pursuits, both in growing closer to God and in helping others along the way.

One more observation: the inseparable verb that works hand in glove with disciple is "grow." We repeatedly find Jesus employing agrarian analogies that evoked vivid images for his hearers, and these images translate today, too. Let me say it again: we are to grow in discipleship and to help others in grow in theirs. This growth calls for seed planting, fertilization, all manner of cultivation (care and feeding), pruning (ouch), and prayer.

Actually, it gets even more basic than that. In the beginning—the very beginning, THE beginning—God created man. Adamah is the Hebrew word for earth, thus Adam translates as earth-creature, he who is created from the earth. And like all creations who come from the earth, we are designed for growth. If we are to blossom into our full potential, we must be cultivated. God ordained Adam to cultivate the garden even as he cultivated Adam. And in the same manner, God continues to cultivate us today.

Disciple is indeed a verb. You are called into a discipleship that includes intentionally discipling others to grow in faith and incorporates being discipled as you grow in your own faith. It is a journey we never finish in this life, instead only reaching its full potential when God completes us in the next life.

Discipling is active.

Discipling is intentional.

Discipling takes effort.

Walk with me as we explore God's calling to make disciples of all nations.

Yes, disciple is a verb.

CHAPTER 1
Your Call to Discipleship

> *Coming to him, a living stone, rejected indeed by men, but chosen by God, precious. You also, as living stones, are built up as a spiritual house, to be a holy priesthood, to offer up spiritual sacrifices, acceptable to God through Jesus Christ. Because it is contained in Scripture, "Behold, I lay in Zion a chief cornerstone, chosen, and precious: He who believes in him will not be disappointed."*
>
> 1 Peter 2:4-6

> "The call to discipleship is the particular summons by which Jesus discloses and reveals himself to individuals in order to claim and sanctify them as his own, and as his witness to the world. Jesus is seeking people to serve him."
>
> *Karl Barth*

God is calling you.

Yes, you.

He most certainly is!

God has a purpose for each person he creates—actually, for every one of his creations—mineral, plant, or animal. And you are one of his masterpieces.

God had a unique purpose in mind as he created each of us, and it is our charge to discern what work we are to accomplish and to get after it. The great Biblical commentator of the mid-20th century, William Barclay, said, "There are two great moments in a man's life. The first is when he was born; the second is when he discovers why he was born."

The first obstacle in discerning our purpose is our denial. Do any of these excuses sound familiar?

> God can't use me.
> God surely can't use me as I am.
> I have to clean up my act before I can be of any use to God.
> God cannot overcome what I did [recalling some great sin or shortcoming]; he will never trust me again.

These are all lies of the Great Deceiver, the Father of All Lies. He wants you to shrink from the greatness for which you were created. One of the great powers of prayer is the ability to drown out that voice in your head that constantly tells you, "You can't." Casting Crowns has a great song, "The Voice of Truth," in which the giant constantly assures you you'll never win, but

The voice of truth says, "Do not be afraid!"
And the voice of truth says, "This is for My glory"
Out of all the voices calling out to me,
I will choose to listen and believe the voice of truth.[3]

Not only do we get to choose, but we must choose. We can listen to the voice of defeat or we can listen to the Voice of Truth. Part of the discipline which Paul decreed by imploring us to pray unceasingly is to pray down the voice of defeat and weakness and to pray up the voice of God that reminds us he created us for a great work and he reminds us he *will never leave nor forsake us.*

This was a constant challenge for me until several years ago when my church offered a short course directed at helping individuals discern their true design. The idea was that by learning our spiritual gifts and passions, we could direct our efforts into the areas of ministry where we would be most effective (a curriculum developed by Bill Hybels and his extremely talented team at Willow Creek Baptist Church[4]).

One of the exercises in the course required me to invite 5-10 friends who knew me well to review a list of spiritual gifts, and pick the three they most closely associated with me, the premise being that friends will often see in a person what the person can't see on his/her own. As Roy H. Williams observes, "It's hard to read the label when you're inside the bottle."[5]

All but one of my respondents chose Faith in my top three and the most of them listed it first on the list. I was astonished! There was no way Faith could be a strength of mine, since I am always seeking ways to improve in this area of personal weakness.

As is typical of me, I shared my incredulousness with my wife, who in turn said, "Of course it is, they are completely right!" which is perfectly typical of her. Not willing to accept her word for it (which is perfectly typical of me), I shared it with our Sunday school class the next week, to widespread shaking of heads and assent with the assessment. The most common sentiment expressed was, "Duh!"

Now, overlay that experience with a recurring observation of hers. "How can someone with so much faith be so afraid?" she says as she looks me in the eye. It is a bit of a conundrum, but it all tracks back to which voice I choose to listen to. I truly, sincerely, deeply believe the message of the "Voice of Truth" song, but at times I fail to drown out the voice that constantly reminds me of my failures.

The second obstacle is choosing not to listen. A very helpful image here involves television transmissions. Television stations broadcast constantly and the waves constantly swirl around us, but we don't notice them until we turn on a TV. Today, we are virtually swimming in a sea of waves—television, radio, microwave, cell phone, internet, the Cloud. Similarly, God is constantly communicating with us and it is up to us to dial into his broadcasts.

A third obstacle to heeding God's call on your life is trying to do it all. One of the most confounding scriptures for me for the longest time was Isaiah 40:31, *But those who wait for Yahweh will renew their strength. They will mount up with wings like eagles. They will run, and not be weary. They will walk, and not faint.* It seemed to me to have been written in reverse. Surely you had to walk before you could run and soaring had to come way later, but then a pastor made sense of it for me.

He observed that when we first come to Christ we soar. We are completely intoxicated by this new relationship with our feet barely touching the ground. Once we spiritually return to earth, we are full of energy running here and there telling everyone we meet about this new life in Christ. We sign up for every ministry and mission endeavor that comes our way. Eventually though, we tire and slow down. It is in this controlled, patient, obedient manner that we truly walk with Jesus and cultivate the fruit of the spirit. When I take time to assess where God can best use me, he provides the strength and stamina to see it through.

In this first phase (spiritual soaring) you soak it all up, swimming in the faith. It is in the second phase (spiritual running), you are vulnerable to trying to do it all. If you don't rein it in, you are destined for spiritual burnout. Remember, you were uniquely designed for a specific purpose, and no one has all the spiritual gifts. No one has all the required resources to meet the vast needs of the world.

Another segment of the Hybels spiritual gifts course was targeted at identifying my passions. Once I determined where I find joy and where I excel, these insights greatly impacted my faith walk, but the more valuable lesson was where my passions and gifts do not exist.

I learned no one should ever trust me with a hammer in my hand... and I learned yet another important lesson. I should never feel guilty for not participating in endeavors for which I am ill-equipped. Actually, the church is much better off when I stay away from those projects.

Up until that epiphany, I felt a pang of guilt whenever there was a workday at the church, or when the "men of the church" fanned out in the community for carpentry and repair projects. As uncomfortable as I felt in my feeble efforts at repairs of that nature, those men felt equally uncomfortable standing in front of a class with lesson in hand. No kingdom purpose is served when I frustrate myself in endeavors for which I was not designed.

Hear me clearly! I was not designed to operate power tools or swing a hammer. Whenever I need affirmation of that belief, I only need to ask my wife! I was designed to comb the scriptures, sit at the feet of Biblical scholars, and to relate those teachings to those who haven't the time (or interest) to invest similarly. I now devote myself where I can be effective and leave to others whose natural design equips them to handle physical work. They are meant to take on those critically worthwhile endeavors without my interference.

David Augsburger in his book, *Dissident Discipleship*, posed a great series of escalating questions when confronted with these opportunities:

What would Jesus do?
What did Jesus do?
What would Jesus have me do?
What is Jesus doing here among us?
What do I do with Jesus?
Jesus, what do you want me to do?[6]

I find it fascinating that Augsburger asked all the other questions first before arriving at, "Jesus, what do you want me to do?" That's me to a T. I ask every question imaginable before posing the one question with which I should have started!

A fourth obstacle is peering into the future in an effort to make sense of it all. You want to know what the end game is, or rather how the game ends. What will you accomplish? Where is this path leading you? How does it all fit into God's plan? Where is God's plan leading you?

This is common to most folks. We want to know where we fit in the larger scheme of things, but I turn to a fabulous word picture created by N. T. Wright. He invites us to envision a young apprentice stonecutter working in the yard of what is in the process of becoming a 15th century castle/cathedral. The master stonecutter has provided him a stone and instructions of what he needs the young man to produce—a block of stone of precise dimensions, specific edges with a determined design. The apprentice's job is to produce just such a stone.

The apprentice doesn't comprehend where it will go in the building or what purpose it will serve, but he knows what he is to carve. What matters is that he produce what the master stonecutter requested. The master stonecutter has already designed where it will go in the structure, how the sides must fit with the stones on either side of it, and how the pattern aligns with the others in that area to create the desired mural. That information is not helpful to the apprentice. He merely needs to recognize that he has a block to carve and that the block is important in the construction of the castle/cathedral.

Similarly, God wants each of us to accomplish specific things in bringing his kingdom. It is not important for us to fathom how the kingdom will be accomplished or how our involvement advances it. We merely need to identify what he requires of us and how to bring our talents to bear, and believe that our work is indeed critical to bringing his kingdom. The Master will take it from there. Just like the apprentice who may or may not ever see the completed structure or where his block resides, we may or may not see the finalization of God's kingdom on earth and how our contributions fit.

This is yet another area where I have to remain attentive at all times. I so want to understand what it is I am to accomplish and discover the path to get there. As has always been his way, Jesus says, *Follow Me*. He wants me to trust him and embark on the journey, to trust him as the path unfolds before me, little by little as I make my way along by following him.

With that thought in mind, I turn to John 21:20-23:

Then Peter, turning around, saw a disciple following. This was the disciple whom Jesus loved, the one who had also leaned on Jesus' breast at the supper and asked, "Lord, who is going to betray You?" Peter, seeing him, said to Jesus, "Lord, what about this man?"

Jesus said to him, "If I desire that he stay until I come, what is that to you? You follow me." This saying therefore went out among the brothers, that this disciple wouldn't die. Yet Jesus didn't say to him that he wouldn't die, but, "If I desire that he stay until I come, what is that to you?"

This is yet another scripture I found confusing for a very long time, until I discovered an interpretation that resonated with me. The interpreter offered that Peter is inquiring about the fate of his friend John, to which Jesus compassionately replies that what becomes of John is between God and John, and what becomes of Peter is between God and Peter.

This passage falls immediately on the heels of Jesus' call to Peter to feed his lambs and to take care of his sheep. While somewhat obtuse, John's message to us in citing this exchange between Jesus and Peter is a directive to us. Jesus calls you to work with him to bring his kingdom. What he requires of you is not the same as what he requires of your boss, your spouse, your children, or your neighbor... and most certainly not what he commands of your pastors.

This brings me to the fifth, final, and maybe the most significant obstacle. We have been duped into believing it is the job of the clergy to feed us spiritually, to do the work of the Lord, while our job is to feast on what they provide. In so doing, we become nourished and fulfilled people. This is not what Jesus taught or intended.

It's so easy (and so common) to say, "I am justa..." Each of us can fill in the blank. Justa teacher, businessman, engineer, firefighter, stay-at-home mom or dad, attorney. We hide behind the fact we are not ordained and have little to offer since we are Justa Whatever. This malady has no end.

Charles Barkley at the height of his NBA career said he wasn't a role model, observing, "I'm just an athlete." There are few higher profile occupations in modern America than professional athlete. What better profession to model Christian beliefs and actions than from that high-exposure profile?

But it isn't just athletes and celebrities. Every single one of us is in a position to model the life of Christ for someone every day, yet rarely are we aware of this wide and diverse audience that constantly watches us.

I'm a financial accountant by training and for the longest time I saw my job as keeping the books in balance, producing monthly financial reports, measuring financial performance to budgets, and making financial presentations. One Sunday, our preacher woke me up to the realization that I too had a ministry, and it wasn't off in the future somewhere. It was right then and right there in that work environment.

When I began to regard my work as a ministry, it took on a much broader scope and I realized my responsibility was much greater. I became responsible for the care and development of everyone around me, seeking ways to make their jobs easier.

Note that I said everyone. It was not limited to people who reported to me on the organization chart or on my team or in my department or my boss. Everyone around me.

Reread 1 Peter 2, with particular attention to verses 4-5 and 9-10. *You also, as living stones, are built up as a spiritual house, to be a holy priesthood, to offer up spiritual sacrifices, acceptable to God through Jesus Christ.*

Then, *But you are a chosen race, a royal priesthood, a holy nation, a people for God's own possession, that you may proclaim the excellence of him who called you out of darkness into his marvelous light: who in time past were no people, but now are God's people, who had not obtained mercy, but now have obtained mercy.*

We are called into ministry, to be part of this priesthood, a holy and royal priesthood. Mark Buchanan encapsulated it for me in his book, *The Holy Wild,* "Sunday after Sunday, I speak to the people about God. Week after week, I speak to God about the people."[7]

That sounds like a major undertaking, but when I stop and think it through, I know I can live up to that calling. Each Sunday, whether teaching a lesson, participating in a lesson brought by someone else, or just passing others in the hall, I have the opportunity to talk to the people about God. I can choose to do so, or hold back. During the week, I have the opportunity to talk to God about the people (constantly). It's called prayer. I can pray for them, or I can refrain. God calls me to engage on both fronts. People rely on me to engage. When I withhold, I hurt them, I hurt myself, and I hurt God.

Now admittedly, many of us are uncomfortable taking "God into the workplace," and in some environments it is strictly forbidden. I know this firsthand from working in administration for a public school system for several years. Even though I was not in a classroom or in a school building, expressions of religious beliefs were frowned upon in ways you can't imagine. While I acknowledged and respected the rules, it did not mean I could not be Christian in thought and deed, if not directly in word.

I consciously carried Christ in my heart into the workplace every day. I did not pepper my conversations scripture. I did not decorate my office with religious art or faith reminders. I did not organize prayer meetings. I did, however, treat everyone with compassion. I did keep a cross in a discreet place on my desk with the inscription "Walk in the Light." I did become a trusted person providing a safe place where people could come for comfort and strength, or, if for nothing else, just to be heard. I was not embarrassed or ashamed by my faith. I did, however, temper my zeal to fit the situation.

Some will tell you I didn't fulfill the calling of

Christ because I was not more outspoken about faith, seeking to share the Gospels in outward ways, and they may have an argument. But I assure you I helped more people, ministered to more hurting souls there than I did when I was working on the staff of a church. Had I been more overt in expressing my Christianity in the school environment, I would have had a very short tenure with the organization and the needs of those hurting people would likely have gone unattended.

Working on the administrative staff of a wonderful, caring church was incredibly inspiring and uplifting. I was surrounded by like-minded people directly serving in God's presence every day. God's hands were evident every day, but he was equally engaged with me when serving the school system.

Our most effective Christian messages are delivered not in pulpits and not with open Bible in hand, but rather through the message we send through our actions and in being accessible to those in need as we go about our daily business.

Let's be perfectly clear here. This calling is not just for the ordained. We are all called. It's time each of us come to this realization, accept the call, and begin actively looking for where God needs us in his service.

Rather than close this chapter on an obstacle, let me remind you that God resides within you. He resides within each and every person on the earth. Some have buried God's presence under a mound of dirt and earthly pursuits, but it still exists within even them. In those who have sought relationship with God though, it burns brightly. And amazingly, he offers more than just a relationship. He offers us friendship, true friendship.

Jesus said to his disciples in John 15:15, *No longer do I call you servants, for the servant doesn't know what his lord does. But I have called you friends, for everything that I heard from my Father, I have made known to you.* While they were his direct audience, he speaks to us across the ages as well.

David Lowes Watson said it this way, "Jesus challenges us to become his disciples in preparing for God's salvation of the world, and he promises us the privilege of his friendship. Moreover, this is the offer of a true friendship—a sharing of everything."[8]

We have now addressed listening for God's call on our lives, his special purpose for our lives and how to put it to work wherever we are, whatever we do. Reviewing our exploration thus far, we find a series of descriptors. Now, let's turn our attention to defining this word disciple.

Disciple is a verb!

STUDY QUESTIONS

Is the idea hard to accept that God calls you? If so, why? Which of the denial obstacles ring true for you?

God can't use me.

God surely can't use me as I am.

I have to clean up my act before I can be of any use to God.

God cannot overcome what I did recalling some great sin or shortcoming; he will never trust me again.

Can you identify specific times in your life when you felt God called you? What would you share about those times?

What methods have you found helpful in amplifying the Voice of Truth and in quieting the voices of defeat?

In what ways do you feel effective in ministry? Are there areas where you feel ill-equipped? Do you feel guilty in not joining in for those work areas?

32 ♀ Robert McBurnett

CHAPTER 2

What is a Disciple?

Jesus answered them, "The time has come for the Son of Man to be glorified. Most certainly I tell you, unless a grain of wheat falls into the earth and dies, it remains by itself alone. But if it dies, it bears much fruit. He who loves his life will lose it. He who hates his life in this world will keep it to eternal life. If anyone serves me, let him follow me. Where I am, there will my servant also be. If anyone serves me, the Father will honor him."

John 12:23-26

Programmatically, Bonhoeffer notes, "Follow me are Jesus' first and last words to Peter." Perhaps they are Christ's first and last words to any and every disciple.

David Augsburger

Disciple is indeed a verb, and we'll get to that quickly, but for the moment consider:

Disciple, *n. one who follows.*

One. Who. Follows. Jesus favorite invitation was "Follow Me." I count no less than 15 instances in the gospels alone where Jesus invites people to follow him, not counting the "Come and sees." You will recall Follow Me is the invitation he extended in calling out the men who would become his twelve disciples. It is also the invitation he extended to the rich young ruler. He implores people to take up their crosses daily and *follow me.* And most gloriously, Jesus reminds Peter twice in their final earthly meeting, *You must follow m*e.

His two simple words are a charge that rings down the ages.

The first step in becoming a disciple in any regard is choosing whom you will follow. Maybe you keep up with your favorite football team, or a favorite musical performer. Many people choose to be disciples of a powerful politician or leader. You can also choose to practice a discipline or lifestyle. Each of these can take on different levels of intensity, from mild interest to using these teachings and examples in transforming every part of your life.

While we are called to be many things, we are called first and foremost to become Jesus' disciples and to follow him. Those who do will find him to be the most powerful of all leaders, and they discover answering his call brings discipline to live a life fashioned after his. The choice is yours. Choose to follow mildly, merely taking notice of his presence in the world, or choose to recommit to redesign your life after his teachings and examples. You get to choose!

Slow down and read that again. You choose: follow mildly or become committed in full to his teachings and examples. You choose.

Remember also that God constantly calls you. You, however, retain the power to choose: choose to ignore, choose to answer, or choose to serve. The choice is entirely yours, but choose you must.

I'll take you back to the opening of this chapter, where I noted that you can follow a sports team, or musician, or politician, or any of a myriad of disciplines and lifestyles. It's not that you must choose between Jesus and those other options. You have to choose Jesus above those other options.

When I chose Jesus, I didn't abandon following my favorite sports teams, I just began scheduling my prayer times and service to others first and then slotted time for the sporting events. I didn't cart my music collection down to the used bookstore and sell it, nor did I reprogram all the presets on my car radio to Christian stations. I did, however, expand my music collection to include numerous Christian artists and set the first two buttons in my car to Contemporary Christian stations. These are examples and are in no way indicative of the choices you are called to make.

I found the more I exposed myself to Christian music, however, the more it moved me, and the more it moved me, the more I wanted to listen to it. At first, I listened to the same artists I always had (ZZ Top, Willie Nelson, Matchbox 20, etc.) and sprinkled in a little Christian Rock (Casting Crowns and Third Day are my personal favorites). Over time, I gravitated more and more towards Christian music and now I listen predominately to Christian Rock and sprinkle in the secular music on occasion. The priority has been reversed, not because it was somehow mandated, but rather because the more I received, the more I wanted. It was indeed a choice I made over time.

Which brings us to the next aspect: intentionality. You can make specific, conscious decisions or you can just amble along. Jesus, however, looks for you to make an intentional decision to follow him.

I well remember reading one of those time

management experts one evening who wrote, "If it's not on your calendar, it's not going to happen and you need to commit time to your marriage. Make sure you schedule at least one date night a month with your spouse." Those might not be the precise words, but you've heard similar messages, I imagine. Silly me, I laughingly read it to my wife, saying we had been having monthly dates for years.

Now, it was her turn to laugh and it wasn't a humorous laugh, but rather a derisive one. Not wise enough to avoid treading into this enchanted forest, I whipped out my calendar and recited all my events and appointments.

Very quickly I learned two lessons. First, not everything I considered a date counted as one. By way of examples, no outing that included our kids, or was in any way related to my company, qualified as a date. Second, our dating frequency was not what I thought it was. A course correction followed.

So, here again I learned that what I thought occurred naturally didn't really come to pass unless I intentionally caused it to happen.

For a long, long time, I was quite content to amble along Discipleship Road. Jesus called me when I was ten and I made the conscious choice right then to begin following him. From that decision forward, I was on the path.

Unfortunately, I merely rambled along the path, void of intentionality for decades. I followed the basic tenets of the faith and I knew all my Sunday school Bible lessons. I kept the Ten Commandments (at least whenever it was convenient) and dabbled in prayer and church attendance, but that was pretty much the extent of it. Like so many followers of Christ, I failed to realize the significant difference between church attendance and true discipleship.

I won't tell you it didn't serve me well, because I was living a life of integrity and I had the assurance that comes from knowing God; however, my faith was not benefiting others. There was no dimension of service there. There was no intensity in my efforts to know Jesus or God. I was a very passive Christian.

It wasn't until I made a purposeful decision to get serious about following him that I began to have an impact. Similar to the gravitation of my musical choices outlined above, I sought new ways to encounter Jesus. This increased interest grew into a hunger and thirst for a relationship with God. I read the Bible voraciously to understand how it all fit together and to what purposes it could be applied. I learned that the "end" it sought was for me to be in a direct, personal relationship with God - to learn everything I could about him; to talk with him daily and throughout each day; to seek his will in my life; and to seek opportunities to serve others.

This marked the turning point from being a follower to becoming a disciple. Shortly thereafter, I realized my pursuit of mediocrity left me far short of God's expectations.

You see, the whole Bible builds to a single overarching message and that message is to follow God's son. More succinctly, to hear Jesus say, "Follow Me" and to heed the call. It starts with following which calls for an intentionality that leads to discipleship.

I grappled with what it means to be a disciple, and then I found David Watson's marks of a disciple in his book, *Called and Committed, World Changing Discipleship*:

> willing to serve
> learning to listen
> willing to learn
> teachable
> submissive to authority
> willing to share his/her faith with others
> learning humility; examines his/her own life
> knows his/her own weaknesses and allows God's grace to work through them
> is not a perfectionist

> forgiving
> persistent, courageous, not easily discouraged
> trustworthy, responsible; not a busybody
> does things well, uses time wisely
> aims to please God most of all
> is quick to obey when God speaks
> has faith in God
> is willing to trust the love and faithfulness of God
> willing to follow where the Spirit is leading
> and has an understanding of God's priorities.[9]

I find his list well defines what we strive to become when we grow as disciples of Christ, provided we have a heart for the Lord and fix our eyes on Jesus.

As I read this list, I see three emergent themes.

Openness to being recreated: Teachability, willingness to learn, learning to listen, aims to please God, and willingness to follow where the Spirit leads are all indicative of being open to God's transformative powers. I hear the strains of the sacred chorus:

> *Spirit of the living God,*
> *Fall afresh on me.*
> *Melt me, mold me,*
> *Make me, use me.*[10]

Trust in God: Submission to authority, allows

God's grace to work through them, persistent, courageous, not easily discouraged, has faith in God, is willing to trust the love and faithfulness of God and quick to obey when God speaks fall in this category. Here again, I'm back in my hymnal. This time hearing "When We Walk With the Lord":

> *Trust and obey,*
> *For there's no other way*
> *To be happy in Jesus,*
> *But to trust and obey.*[11]

Take action for the Kingdom: Willingness to serve, willingness to share one's witness, forgiving, does things well, and uses time wisely are all calls to action.

Being a disciple involves so much more than just digesting doctrine and scripture. It isn't about winning arguments about your faith. In the words of Bob Goff, "I don't want to be right any more. I just want to be Jesus." It's about taking on a mindset that leads to constantly thinking in Christ-like ways.

Reaching back to Deuteronomy 6:6-9, "And these words which I command you today shall be in your heart. You shall teach them diligently to your children, and shall talk of them when you sit in your house, when you walk by the way, when you lie down, and when you rise up. You shall bind them as a sign on your hand, and they shall be as frontlets between your eyes. You shall write them on the doorposts of your house and on your gates, not in the literal way adopted by the rabbis," always in the forefront of our minds, living out the words of his teachings. Paul picks up the theme repeatedly imploring us to transform our minds and to think, think, think like Christ.

We need to start with embracing the truth that the spirit of God, the Holy Spirit, resides within each of us. Some of us have shoved it so far in the background that it is all but indiscernible. The Bible assures us we are created in God's image; nevertheless, we can reject the image of God through our exercise of choice (otherwise known as human free will), and in so doing regress into an animalistic nature. As I contemplate people I know who choose to live primarily for the rewards of this world rather than to seek the life God calls us to, they seem to take on animalistic traits—satiating physical needs, survival of the fittest, care only for self, grabbing all they can reach. If you choose to pursue the fruits of the world, God's spirit retreats within you, not because of some decision God made, but rather as a result of yours. I also believe God honors our decisions, no matter how much our choices grieve him.

If, on the other hand, we choose to feed God's spirit within us, it increases like the mustard seed in

Mark 4 that "grows up, and becomes greater than all the herbs, and puts out great branches, so that the birds of the sky can lodge under its shadow." And from that growth, Paul's fruit of the spirit emerges (love, joy, peace, patience, kindness, generosity, faithfulness, gentleness, and self-control).

I look back across my career and see the fruits of these two divergent paths. I see the concentration on pursuit of worldly rewards. The areas of our society where the pursuit of worldly gain is most on display might well be with athletes, entertainers, and politicians. I devoted most of my business career to professional sports administration, which provided me a unique insight into the allure of these worldly fruits. The call to amass power and wealth, and to feed one's natural instincts for food, booze, and sex is strong. I do not attribute this phenomenon to weak character in athletes. It lives within us all.

Professional athletes succumb to these urges primarily due to time and access. They have a lot of discretionary time to fill between practices and games, and if they are successful at their trade, money flows their way. Those are powerful magnets for others (disciples of a different sort) who want to present even more opportunities to the athlete. It is a heady spiral, incredibly hard to resist. In that light, it is easy to see how trouble seems to pursue them.

Entertainers and politicians fall into similar patterns as a result of temptations where time and access are prevalent. My observation is not that these individuals are of weak character, rather that they are exposed to allures the rest of us will never understand.

On the other hand, I have seen many athletes and musicians who took a different path, who saw their abilities as a means to put their talents, time, and access to work for a higher cause. I say "higher cause" on purpose. Many take every opportunity to "give God the glory" and to "thank Jesus my savior." It is uplifting to hear them draw people's attention to God and encouraging their fans and followers to be drawn to study God and Jesus. I've also witnessed celebrities go out of their way to be true disciples of Christ, seeking opportunity after opportunity to serve others and to help those that most need help.

Many athletes (and entertainers and politicians) are quick to step out in Christian service, many more than is ever publicized. I know several ballplayers who took on virtuous service on the condition that there would be no media presence or public acknowledgment. But it didn't end there. Scores of others were "doing the right thing" without any clue they were answering God's call. How many times did I hear, "It was nothing man. He/She/They just needed some help."?

Many were great examples who intentionally lived for Jesus, yet others were just strolling along God's path, or had yet to choose, but all nevertheless lent a hand in bringing God's love and healing into the world around them. Each had an impact in making the world a better place. Yet those who made the conscious choice to be disciples made a kingdom difference.

I tell these stories to highlight our lack of discretion in choosing whom we model our lives after. Most often, it is not a conscious decision at all. We simply mimic the behavior of those with whom we associate, or those whose exploits and achievements attract us. We acclimate to our surroundings. We become like those with whom we spend the most time. In this context, the "spending time" need not be in person. I spend time with all my favorite sports teams, even though I may never meet anyone on the team or even in the organization.

I remember a time in my life when I worked very hard to make my organization successful. I poured everything into ensuring we never missed a deadline and never fell short of expectations. Eventually, it overwhelmed me and I couldn't keep up. I rapidly came to the conclusion that this just wasn't going to work. Little did I know that my boss had reached the same conclusion about me.

We met and he suggested maybe I should consider leaving the company. He offered to broker an agreeable arrangement with the top of the managerial pyramid. I went home that evening and discussed it with my wife, telling her it was time for me to go. To my surprise, she agreed. When I came home the next evening after accepting the offer, I felt as though I had let the family down. I apologized to her only to hear her say, "I am so relieved. You were becoming someone I didn't like." Now those are words you never want to hear from your spouse, let me assure you!

I had mimicked the behavior of those around me in the organization and it had transformed me into someone she didn't like. I had adapted to my work environment. I had complied with the expectations of the organization directly at the expense of my family responsibilities and, on reflection, in conflict with my core Christian beliefs. It was not a choice I made purposefully. I had conceded to the demands and expectations of the work environment by default. (I will also acknowledge that the negative aspects of this work environment were much of my own creation.) I never intended to turn my back on my family or my core Christian beliefs, but I had set my sights on being successful in that context and lost sight of the other calls on my life.

I remind you, we are not called to be successful, rather we are called to be faithful. I had focused on the wrong one.

So now we shift our focus to whom it is we follow. I challenge you to stop right now and make a list of the people you admire. Write down your list. Don't list three or four and call it good. Think across all aspects of your life. Don't leave out any segments. Flush out several people in each area—work, neighbors, lifelong friends and acquaintances, church, athletes and celebrities, even people you've never met who have an impact on the person you are.

Seriously! Stop and compile it mentally right now and put it down on paper before reading on. I'll wait.

Now, reflect on what it is you admire about each of them—their success, their looks, their integrity, their commitment to others? What aspects of their behavior have you incorporated into your personality? And here's the big one—are they truly worthy of your emulation?

Once you get it all on paper, set it aside, but let it simmer in your subconscious. Go back to the list tomorrow and see what other attributes and names come to mind. Then give it another look in a week.

Get a good thorough list.

Now, return to Zechariah 8:23 with me. Acknowledge you are indeed attached to someone's robe, and more likely to more than one robe. I feel very safe in saying there are a few select people on your list to whose robes you are attached. Be deliberate about to whom you attach yourself. Don't hasten off too quickly and fail to address two questions. Who is it you are following? and What about them is worthy of your emulation?

If I am not intentional about why I'm following someone's lead, I merely fall into a pattern of behavior that enhances success, and all too often that success is in the eyes of the world, but is not faithful to God. This will come as no surprise to you, but not everyone in the business world is following in the paths of righteousness.

Hear me carefully here. I'm not saying the business world is corrupt, because I definitely don't see it that way. Some within the business community are indeed corrupt, but most business people are honest and straightforward. Nor am I saying success in the business world is a sign of departure from God's path. Quite the contrary. We are called to be faithful wherever we are, and for many of us it is in the business world. Following God and succeeding in the business world are not incompatible if you do it right. Fix your eyes daily on God and on those who do likewise. They are right in front of you for a reason.

These are not casual options, either. They are commitments. Iron-willed commitments. In Luke 9, Jesus steadfastly set his face to go to Jerusalem. Going to Jerusalem was the one thing that dominated his thoughts and plans from then on. This is not to say that he shut out everything else, though. Between making this commitment and his arrival in Jerusalem, he cast out demons, healed a blind man, met Zacchaeus and the rich young ruler, enlightened Mary and Martha about the greatest thing, taught the disciples how to pray, sent out the 70 disciples (and then received them back), and shared parable after parable... among other things. Jesus demonstrated that we can fix our eyes steadfastly on what is primary, yet remain attentive to God's people and their needs along the way.

But seek first God's Kingdom, and his righteousness; and all these things will be given to you as well, Matthew 6:33 tells us. Fix your mind on God's plan, and fix your eyes on those you willfully seek to follow down his path. Then, watch for the multitude of opportunities that occur along this path for you to serve God's children. All God's children, every child for whom Jesus gave his life.

I can't say it more clearly than this – Be intentional! Yes, there are times to take your time and amble along, but never lose sight of the primary purpose of your journey.

And yet I caution you not to go too far with this idea of intentionality. Our society makes it so easy to fall in the trap of planning every step or your journey, every minute of your day. Leave room for God to participate.

Not surprisingly, Jesus gave us a prime example. Both Mark and Luke record the story of Jairus' daughter, who lies dying. Jairus implores Jesus to heal his daughter and Jesus departs with him immediately only to be detained by the woman with the twelve-year issue of blood. Jesus is fixated on saving Jairus' daughter, a most urgent matter, yet he stops to heal this woman on his way to Jairus' house. It's not a passing encounter either. He stops, makes inquiries of the crowd, and then engages the woman in an intimate conversation.

Nothing noted in the scripture provides details of this exchange, but in my mind's eye, this emerges as one of the tenderest moments in the gospels when he helps her up from the ground and peers deeply into her eyes. Yes, Jesus demonstrates for us that nothing can be so urgent we can't stop along the way to meet the needs of a hurting child of God.

As a friend of mine frequently reminds me, "Man plans and God laughs." Leave room in your plans for God to participate.

As is so often the case, my thoughts turn to Peter. Oh, how I relate to Peter, the Peter of the gospels… not to be mistaken with the New Peter that emerges after Pentecost.

Peter experienced the most magnificent view of Jesus' glorious ministry. Peter was one of the first to be called. In Matthew 4, Jesus invites Peter, *Follow me.*

Over the next three years, Peter observed the lame walk, the blind see, the deaf and dumb hear and speak, and he even saw the dead raised to life. Peter watched as Jesus challenged the institutions of the day and rebuked their leaders. Peter saw demons extracted from their dwellings and banished. Peter noted how the mighty were humbled while the poor and outcasts were exalted. Peter participated with Jesus when Moses and Elijah in their glorified spiritual bodies joined them on top of a mountain.

It wasn't just what he saw, either. Peter experienced. Peter lived. Peter was the first to declare Jesus to be the Christ. Peter climbed out of the boat and walked to Jesus across the water. Peter received the keys to the kingdom from Jesus.

Peter also failed. Over and over in the gospels, Peter is the first to step up and take a stand. Over and over, Jesus calls him down. Peter tries repeatedly to live out his faith in Jesus only to fall short again and again. Sinking into the sea as he walked to Jesus, shearing off Malchus' ear in the Garden of Gethsemane, and his denial of Christ in the temple courtyard all come quickly to mind.

We see Peter rising to the highest highs and plunging to the lowest lows over the course of his three-year walk with Jesus. It all ended with the lowest of lows in the temple courtyard when a rooster signaled his failure and (in Luke) Jesus locked him in his gaze in the moment.

But wait... there was more. It wasn't the end after all. Jesus had another ending in mind. Jesus' version of Peter's story resumes on the beach of the Sea of Tiberius with breakfast cooked by the Master, Peter's restoration, and a new charge from Jesus to look after God's people.

Max Lucado said it oh so succinctly in *Six Hours One Friday*, "Our lives are not futile. Our failures are not fatal. Our deaths are not final."[12] One need not look any further than Peter for proof and for an amazing example of discipleship.

From studying the gospels, I ascertain that Jesus'

first message to Peter was *Follow me* (Matthew 4:19) and his parting words to Peter were also *Follow me.* (John 21:19 and 22)

Chose whom you will follow. Make an intentional decision. Recommit to it at the beginning of each day. Expect to stumble, but persist in getting up and charging ahead. Call on the Holy Spirit.

In short, be a disciple!

Yes, sometimes disciple is, after all, a noun... but in the final analysis...

Disciple is a verb!

STUDY QUESTIONS

What does the invitation "Follow me" mean to you?

Think of times when you made an intentional decision to follow. Think of times when you followed without a conscious decision. Contrast the outcomes.

Do you believe you can be a committed follower of Jesus without making changes in your life? Do you feel doing so would require you to abandon all your current practices? Friends?

Which aspects of David Watson's disciple profile speak to you? Which ones don't fit your concept of a disciple?

When you made your list of people you follow, did the names come easily or did you have to work at it? Why do you think that was?

Do you leave room in your plan for God to participate?

CHAPTER 3

What Does a Disciple Do?

Now, Israel, what does Yahweh your God require of you, but to fear Yahweh your God, to walk in all his ways, and to love him, and to serve Yahweh your God with all your heart and with all your soul, to keep Yahweh's commandments and statutes, which I command you today for your good? Behold, to Yahweh your God belongs heaven and the heaven of heavens, the earth, with all that is therein. Only Yahweh had a delight in your fathers to love them, and he chose their offspring after them, even you above all peoples, as it is today.

Deuteronomy 10:12-15

The Christian gospel is God's good news for the whole world. The startling truth that shook those first Christian Jews was that "God shows no partiality, but in every nation... everyone who believes in [Jesus] receives forgiveness of sins through his name," and the last words of Jesus before his ascension into heaven had been "go therefore and make disciples of all nations." This was his master plan for the salvation of the world, brilliant in its simplicity but strangely ignored by much of the church through many generations. His disciples were to make disciples who would make disciples, ad infinitum.

David Watson

What does a disciple do?

Loves.

A disciple loves.

A disciple loves the way Jesus loved.

The heart of discipleship, the heart of Jesus' teachings, is love. Love God, love one another, and love yourself.

At its core, discipleship calls for a mental framework that constantly seeks opportunities to share God's love. It fosters an air that is noticeable in your very presence.

Let's look at a few dimensions of the love that marks the disciple.

Love for Others

The primary outward expression of discipleship comes through love for others manifested in acts of love. This love for others is most evident in overt ministry efforts—outreach to the poor and elderly, prison ministries, disaster relief, compassion for those in grief and the like—but it shows itself most often in ways you are likely to overlook.

We have already addressed bringing the heart of Christ into your workplace, and I can't emphasize that one enough. Endless opportunities arise when you set your mind to extending God's love in the workplace. And the best part is that you often get to help others without their even knowing it.

Many of these acts are small and simple. A commercial running on television right now shows a woman who buys a soft drink from a vending machine but the bottle gets stuck. In dismay, she trudges back to her desk. A man of substantial size has watched from his cubicle. He goes to the machine and rocks it from side to side until the beverage drops. He then strolls over and sets it on the corner of her desk and walks away with a big grin on his face. A small and simple, but appreciated, act.

I am not suggesting we should prowl around looking for opportunities to intimidate vending machines, but he gets credit for a) being aware of the needs of those around him and b) taking action. Little things are in your path every day for you as well. Fill the copier bins before starting your day, straighten up the meeting room when you leave a meeting (whether you called the meeting or not), and don't bring liver and onions or last night's seafood entree to warm in the microwave.

Be attentive to big things, too. In today's workplace, there are almost always people who find themselves in a crisis. Maybe they contributed to the situation, maybe not. Either way, offer to help where you can. My experience has been they rarely accept, but make the offer anyway and pitch in where you can. Shoulder some of their tedious assignments and let them concentrate on the major challenges when the workload overwhelms them (which it does for all of us at one time or another). And don't do it in expectation of their reciprocating down the road. That isn't serving, that's just saving up favors for a rainy day.

Sometimes all you can do is hurt for them. This is generally the case when a coworker is going through a personal trial. An old preacher's story tells about a first-grader who was late getting home from school one day (back in the day when children were entrusted to walk home from school unescorted). Her mom asked the reason for her delay and she explained that on the way home she encountered a friend whose dolly had broken and she stopped to help. Her mother said, "Helped? How did you help? Were you able to fix it?" "No," she said, "I just sat on the curb and helped her cry."

Sometimes, most times, we just need someone to sit and help us cry.

Yet in other situations direct action should be taken. Years ago, one of the ladies on my staff came to work distressed one morning. So distressed that even I noticed. (Admittedly, I was not the most sensitive or aware person at the time.) I asked her what troubled her and she shared that she had a surgical procedure scheduled for later in the week and it had her frightened. I sat and listened and empathized and assured her we would cover her work in her absence. I committed to make the time over the next few days to get up to speed on what needed to be accomplished in her absence, and knowing her faith, assured her I would pray for her throughout the ordeal. She was grateful.

An hour or so later, I was in my boss' office and shared the news confidentially with him, knowing full well that he would support us and pray for her as well. Immediately without hesitation he said, "C'mon, let's go pray with her."

I stammered, "What!? Er . . . uh." All else was lost because he was up, out the door, and headed down the hall.

When we got to her office, he entered gently and said to her, "Renee, Robert just shared with me your situation and I wondered if it would okay if we prayed for you?"

She agreed that would be wonderful and looked somewhat puzzled at me. I was more or less on board by then and nodded in her direction only to hear our boss say, "Robert, step over there and put your hand on her shoulder. I'll start and you can finish up."

I'm pretty sure my mind blew a circuit breaker at that point because I never imagined he had praying aloud in mind. Fortunately, he offered to go first, because it allowed me a couple of minutes to get the blood pumping back into my cranium. His prayer was magnificent and during it the Holy Spirit arrived just in time to put a few meaningful words in my mouth.

Never, ever would I have imagined my participating in such a moment in the workplace. Never, ever would he have thought about doing anything less. It is not an age or generational thing, either. You might well envision him as being significantly older and more experienced, when in truth he was much younger than either of us.

I left her office with an amazing sense of calm and joy. Later in the day, she came by my office to let me know our act of kindness was just what she needed and no one had ever given her such a gift. She was now prepared to face the procedure confidently with a sense of peace and with assurance of a positive outcome.

Now, a few observations before we move on from this story. First and foremost, you should remain mindful of respect for personal relations in the modern workplace at all times. My boss asked sincerely and in a non-threatening manner if she would like us to pray for her. Additionally, we approached her in a private setting where she needn't been concerned about the reactions of others. Finally, note that we placed our hands gently on her shoulders and with her permission. Had any of these overtures been unwelcome, severe consequences would have ensued involving Human Resources, as well they should. And above all else, know your company's culture with regard to matters of this nature, as well as the orientation of the individual involved.

But I also want you to focus on what happened here. I listened with compassion and offered her my support and prayers. Admittedly, the suggestion to assume some of her work required some action on my part, but aside from that my commitment was mental and spiritual. In contrast, my boss' reaction was to jump into action and to address the immediate circumstance with everything he had at the moment. As regards the call of Christ, I was a willing follower, while he was the dedicated disciple.

You may well think right now that the most difficult place to express your faith is in the modern workplace. I assure you that living your faith, especially in your work environment, is precisely what God expects from you. I spent seven years as Chief Financial Officer for a public school system. If I could bring Christ with me to work every day there, you can too, right where God has you now.

Sure, overt expressions may be banned in your workplace, but you can still be Christ in that place. You don't have to cite scripture at every opportunity or confront your co-workers with their salvation status. (A friend of mine shared with me the other day about his adjustment in moving from the suburbs to an inner city neighborhood where alternative lifestyles are common. He told me, "I don't approve of your lifestyle!" has proven to be a very ineffective conversation starter.) Yes, Jesus shared biblical teachings in his ministry, but always in an appropriate setting. Most of the time he was simply Jesus to those he encountered.

One more workplace example. Years ago, the oil & gas industry was in a downturn. Now that I think of it, the oil & gas industry alternates between extreme highs and extreme lows, so they are more often than not in a downturn, either in one or headed for one.

In the throes of a downturn, a geophysicist friend of mine shared his frustrations with us in our Sunday school class. He said he couldn't seem to get his work done due to the constant stream into his office of co-workers distraught by the current state of affairs. They were scared, unsure, and worried they would be the next to get let go. In addition, the numerous layoffs in the company had hit his department extremely hard and the demands to bear the additional workload were increasing. He didn't have the heart to send them away, but he too struggled under the additional workload confronting him. He wasn't even the department head, for crying out loud.

In that instant, in a moment of true inspiration, one of our classmates said, "Matt, did it ever occur to you that maybe God put you there to listen to them and to ease their pain?" Matt blinked a couple of times and replied that he had never thought of it that way, to which our friend added, "It sounds like you're pretty good at it too or they wouldn't keep coming back."

Matt later told me this revelation caused a profound change in his attitude. He began to see those co-workers as his primary work responsibility and the geological analyses and reports as secondary. But magically, once he had this change of heart, somehow the work seemed to get done, too. He didn't slack off on the tasks before him; he just began to see a greater responsibility. Matt began to see his calling.

* * * * *

"So," you ask, "how am I to just be Jesus?" First and foremost, show compassion. Listen, really listen, to those who are hurting. (They are all around you. You don't have to go looking for them.)

In any instance where you put the needs of others ahead of your own (all too uncommon in our culture), love will kick in. Our culture tells us that we are to get all we can, maximize our opportunities, and that joy comes through personal gratification. While we tend to think of this a modern development, it is not all that different from the culture Jesus encountered, which is why his overarching message—true joy comes from meeting the needs of others—was so revolutionary to those who heard it then. Today it sounds even more radical.

Maintain your integrity by consistently acting

ethically. Take the moral high ground. When provoked into a senseless debate, walk away. Often, the right path is in knowing when not to speak up. Don't engage in hurtful conversations. In other words, be Jesus.

And you don't have to call attention to it; actually, a high and mighty attitude will undermine your efforts every time. Just be real. Be sensitive. Be Jesus.

For most of my career, my focus was first on what would best benefit the organization and second on what was in it for me. How could I contribute to advancing the organization's goals? What would advance my career? Which were the keys to getting promoted? How could I get ahead/stay ahead of the competition? When was the next promotion most likely to come?

Early in my career, I got some great advice on how to advance. "The best way to succeed is to look for ways to make your boss's job easier, to make him/her look good." This mindset has proved very beneficial in my corporate advancement. Attending to what was good for my boss almost always paid dividends for me personally.

There came a time though, when I started finding my greatest workplace joy in helping others achieve their goals. One day late in my career, a friend shared that his company, a large international firm, decided to embrace the servant leadership model by turning the "serve your boss' needs" concept on its head. The premise was to invert the traditional organizational pyramid by adopting the view that advancing the organization could best be served by bosses who seek to meet the needs of their subordinates. He said folks were skeptical at first, but in the end it proved wildly successful. Not only did productivity improve, but morale did as well.

As counter-intuitive as that sounded, I decided to give it a try. I experimented with it for a while and sure enough realized it presents a definite recipe for success.

Just imagine an organization where every supervisor sees his/her primary function as understanding his/her direct reports' challenges and constantly seeks ways to make their jobs easier; and in turn every manager cultivates that attitude towards the supervisors and every vice president feels that way about the managers. No, you can't force this inverted pyramid approach company-wide (unless you happen to be the CEO, and even then you can't force it on those who resist), but you can start with yourself and with those for whom you are responsible.

I can't help but wonder how different our capitalist society would be if all companies adopted such an approach. I suspect employee turnover would decline, earnings would climb, stock prices would soar, and corporate cultures would improve dramatically. When you get right down to it, my friend's company centered its philosophy squarely in line with the teachings of Jesus. It was just this type of "turning the world upside down" on which Jesus thrived. Seek the least, the last and the lost. Find a way to improve their lot, to meet their needs, and in so doing you will find your deepest needs met as well. I wonder if this company's leadership had any idea they brought Christ into the workplace when they turned the organizational hierarchy on its head!

And here's the even more difficult part—your serving others extends to everyone, and that includes "that person"—you know the one, the one person you find almost impossible to work with. Jesus said we are to love and pray for our enemies, even those that torment us. Bob Goff instructs us to start with the people who creep us out the most.

I have worked for a number of direct supervisors that were difficult at best, so much so that one counselor of mine observed that maybe I subliminally sought out tough bosses. That still sounds a little eerie to me, but nevertheless that was his genuine assessment. I did a poor job of loving them, although

I did pray for them. I prayed, "Lord, please let this man's actions get him fired!" "God, can you get one of us transferred to another division, and right now?" And the standard, "Lord, get me outta here!"

I achieved a perfect score with those prayers. Not a single one was answered.

One day, God reminded me once again of something I didn't want to hear. He asked me to pray for them to succeed and to have a change of heart. More than either of those, he wanted me to pray for my own change of heart that would lead me to different actions that would in turn have a positive impact on them.

I don't know why I decided to give it a try; maybe I had reached the level of despair where nothing else had worked, so why not? "Christian" would certainly not describe that particular workplace environment and it began at the top. Charging in with Bible in hand was not going to be effective, I assure you, so I prayed that, while I knew our leader would continue to reject Jesus, maybe he could see that treating others with fairness and dignity would pay dividends. I prayed that when we met, I would not let his disposition affect my demeanor.

About that time, I stumbled across a scripture that bolstered me in these potentially combative situations: Exodus 14:14, *Remain calm, the Lord will fight for you.* Now, if you go back and read the context of that scripture, you will find the Israelites in a tough situation the likes of which surely you and I will not face ourselves, but the concept applies in a multitude of circumstances. The Lord will fight for you, he fights for you constantly, if you will remain calm and invite him in through prayer.

A similar, intentional shift of focus can also be a game changer in your marriage. I'm reminded of a line from Larry Gatlin's 1970's hit, "Love is Just a Game" with these lyrics, "We're not making love, we're keeping score." The next time you are in an argument with your spouse (or anyone you love for that matter), stop and ask yourself, "Which is more important, building our relationship or winning this argument?"

Let me be clear, there are some arguments for which winning is essential above all else, however, I rarely find that to be the case. But my competitive nature feeds the drive to win every point, every argument, often to my detriment. I realize it would truly be beneficial to lose many of the arguments in which I engage, but it is so very difficult to let go in the moment.

When I listen to young couples in love headed towards marriage, I hear, "She's beautiful. She makes my heart sing. I want to wake up with her for the rest of my life." "He is amazing. He's funny, and so kind. I want to be with him forever."

Don't get me wrong, that's a great place to start, but what if it went something like, "She's the most amazing, beautiful person I've ever met. I just want to make her happy all the time!" or "He is so very special, I just want him to experience the joy I feel when I am with him."? Now, I know that making someone happy—all the time—is wholly unattainable, but how would your life change if your primary focus in your marriage was in meeting your partner's needs rather than having your needs met?

And it's never too late to experience this shift. I've found the more I focus on discerning what my wife wants in any given situation (since she is not the type to come out and tell me), the more enjoyment I find by bringing her joy... it tends to boomerang back to me. Sadly, I also see how seldom I acted in those ways prior to making it an intentional effort, and I realize how much work I have to do to make it come more naturally. I dream of the day when it becomes effortless for me.

Discipleship is a way of life. It penetrates every aspect of your life.

Love God

After centuries of man's seeking the will of God, you would think that loving God would come naturally for us, but such isn't the case, is it? More and more, it seems we are committed to advancing society, which pushes God further and further into the background.

The first four commandments given to Moses directly address love for God (no gods before me; no graven images; don't misuse my name; keep one day a week holy and dedicated to me), which should provide all the motivation necessary for us to constantly express our love for God. When Jesus is asked what the greatest commandment is, he says, "Love the Lord your God with all your heart and with all your soul and with all your mind. This is the first and greatest commandment." God literally chisels it in stone and later Jesus adamantly affirms it. You would think we would have gotten the message.

Yet, this is the area where we sorely need discipling and where we need to intentionally disciple others.

Loving God begins with learning to love what God loves.

So our first question for reflection is, "What is

it that God loves above all?" and the answer comes back, "His children." More than anything else, God loves us and covets a relationship with us. God's created world is one of mystery, and man's history is the story of discovery, experimentation, and more discovery. The more we know, the more we realize just how much remains that we don't know, and it is through this quest to know that we are constantly driven back to God for understanding.

While I believe God does not bring difficulty upon us, I know he uses these life challenges to invite us into conversation with him. Like an earthly father, he aches for us when we are hurting and is gratified when we turn to him for comfort.

I will boldly push it even further. God wants us to challenge and question him. This differs from doubt. This is entering into passionate dialogue with God. I see it modeled in the Biblical example of Job. Job could not find logic or rationale for the treatment he received at the hands of the Satan. Job's natural tendency would have been to give up, collapsing under the weight of his afflictions. Job was entitled to a life of bitterness causing him to turn his back on God, making it day to day bearing his incredible burden.

But no! Job went to God crying out and raging against the injustice he perceived. And God did not turn his back on Job. I would have expected God to dismiss Job and his ranting as insignificant. But no! God deemed Job worthy of a response. At the height of Job's rage, God showed up to explain the mysteries of the cosmos to him. Contrary to popular belief, Job does not ultimately collapse in defeat; Job collapses in awe of God's majesty.

You see, God yearns for us to converse with him in all situations and in all emotional states, and we call these conversations prayer. Prayer is simply conversation in the presence of God.

Paul's command to *pray without ceasing* comes immediately to mind and on the surface appears impossible. How can one possibly sequester oneself in constant prayer? This is quite the opposite of what Paul had in mind. Paul was imploring us to engage in constant conversation in the presence of God at all times, in all places, while at the same time engaging with the world around us. This attitude of prayer invades all of our activities. Yes, it includes praise and adoration for God (clear expressions of love for God), and it includes our intercessory prayers for others. But it also includes our cries for help in times of need; it includes our anguished cries of despair; it encompasses our railing against those things of which we cannot make sense.

Remember, that great night on the banks of the Jabbok River when Jacob wrestled with the angel (or maybe it was God)? Through that experience, God changed his name from Jacob to Israel (wrestles with man and wrestles with God). This was Jacob's finest moment, where he came to know God in the same intimate way I want to experience God. And he limped into his new existence with a constant reminder of this direct encounter with God. He is scarred for life, but scarred in a way that caused him to remain in the new life to which he was called. I can't imagine that Jacob had a single moment in the rest of his life where he wasn't in conversation with God.

In this light we begin to view prayer as an ongoing process of seeking God in all situations as we grow in discernment of what best contributes to bringing God's kingdom on earth. We draw his kingdom closer by channeling the love he pours into us back out into those we encounter, not day to day, but moment by moment.

Next, let's turn out attention to Bible study. When you decide you want to keep up with certain people, their lives and activities, you turn to… Facebook, of course! No? If you want to know their true character, you begin to study their actions and what they say. You can't follow someone if you know nothing about them or what they stand for. When you truly follow, you want to know everything you can. You need to engage in any action that will enhance your knowledge of them (short of stalking, of course). The best way, the absolute best way, is to spend time in their presence.

Your relationship with God is no different... well, except for two things. First, his existence is so immense and eternal that you will never know everything there is to know about him, and second, you have at your disposal an accurate chronicle of his relationship with mankind: the Bible.

The Bible is more accessible today than at any time since the dawn of time. Not only is it available in printed form, it is available online and even on your phone. You can find numerous points of access, many of which are available free of charge.

And the accessibility reaches far beyond the Bible itself. Never in history have there been as many places to turn to reflect on Jesus and his teachings and application of those teachings as what we have at our disposal today. You can turn to any number of Christian blogs, some by common folk not all that different from you (my weekly blog at mcburnettsmusings.wordpress.com is one example). You can engage through books by current Christian writers such as Philip Yancey, John Ortberg, Mark Buchanan, and Max Lucado, who bring the Bible to life in a modern context. You can dive in with the many great theologians of the day, such as N. T. Wright,

Miroslav Volf, and Timothy Keller.

If you really want to immerse yourself in study, courses abound from full-blown enrollment in seminary (numerous courses of study do not lead to ordination, in addition to those that do) to short-term studies offered at most local churches. Even being isolated in a remote location is no longer an insurmountable obstacle with innumerable options available through the Internet, many of which are excellent. No matter what your level of understanding, no matter the level at which you are willing and able to commit, a wide array of options are available to you.

The pastor of one church I attend implores his congregation in each sermon to "take out your Bible, or get it on your phone, and if you don't have a Bible, please go to the back and get one. It is our gift to you." Another pastor at another church I admire frequently invites his attendees, "If you don't have a Bible, please stop in our bookstore on the way out and steal one. Seriously, we are that intent on you having a Bible! PLEASE steal one on your way out."

They are both dead serious, because they don't want anyone being without the word of God. I will also add that both of these churches are known as open, welcoming congregations where membership is merely a formality. These churches reach those who desperately want to know, but don't know how to get started.

As I see it, Bible study comes in two dimensions. The first is deepening your understanding. I just covered that dimension. What these two pastors are doing addresses the second: broadening your reach.

By now, you have probably summarized this section into its most essential components: prayer and Bible study, more commonly known as spiritual disciplines. We'll cover a third spiritual discipline, worship, in the next section.

But first a word about spiritual discipline. Our tendency is to shrink away at the mention of discipline, given its restrictive and binding nature, but hear this. When Jesus presented these disciplines, his disciples received them as life-giving, inspiring, and, dare I say, fun. That may well lie at the core of the popularity and staying power of the 1980s musical Godspell. It was light and fun with a capital F, as it portrayed Christ's walking and teaching in a spirit of joy. JOY!

Do not commit the grievous error of squeezing the fun and joy out of Jesus and his message. These disciplines are designed to bring you deep-seated joy.

Community

We tend to look at prayer and Bible study as personal pursuits, things we do in private. Discipleship and the study of God are not about withdrawing from the world. God's design was and is for us to be in community. We are constantly creating and reshaping society, yet another dimension of being created in the image of God. God created the physical order and looks to us to create the societal order.

Granted, there are times to withdraw in private prayer and study. We need to retreat at times to prepare ourselves to be more effective in community, but only in the interest of preparation.

Imagine a ship. It comes into port for repairs and to restock. The crew goes ashore to get recharged, but the purpose of the ship is not what is accomplished in port; its purpose comes in what is accomplished at sea. We pray and study to prepare and recharge, but our real purpose is to be Jesus in our communities. Our communities are the seas where our real work is accomplished.

These ventures lead us to the outward manifestation of love for God through worship, both private and corporate, and I unabashedly profess it requires both. You can worship in church boldly proclaiming your love for Christ and walk out the door and not think about him again until the next Sunday.

On the other hand, you can worship God through prayer, Bible study, and shouting in the privacy of your home, but never darken the door of a church. Neither is effective without the other. In isolation, one without the other is so ineffective as to be counterproductive.

We were designed for communal worship. Upon emerging from his 40 days preparing for ministry in the desert, Jesus immediately set about calling his disciples and his community grew outwardly from there. Later, Paul described the church as the bride of Christ, underlining Jesus' ministry as one of connectedness.

Now, this is not about building the institution we call "the church." Many of the great wars and conflicts have arisen from the perpetuation and defense of the religious power structure, and I am convinced it grieves God greatly. The "church" here is the community of disciples of Jesus who work for the good of all mankind with the objective of bringing God's reign on earth.

The church community and the corporate worship it offers strengthen us to work in the wider community in which those churches exist. They provide a support system for the inevitable times of trial that come our way. A pastor told of a church member who had been through immense trial who said it this way, "The congregation was able to say the creed for me when I didn't have the strength to say it myself." It is about shoring each other up. As we work through this verb disciple, we will talk more about the power of encouragement, the type of encouragement that comes only through community.

Private worship, on the other hand, builds the spiritual muscle that injects your relationship with Christ into every aspect of your life. It comes through the means we explored above, prayer and Bible study. It comes through constant awareness of the needs around you and the resources you have to offer (we'll talk more about that as we work through the chapters that follow). It is about developing a mindset of gratefulness, what a dear friend of mine refers to as the attitude of gratitude.

Gratitude

Let me share a few concepts regarding this attitude of gratitude. In the realm of prayer, it's expressing thankfulness to God. I admit that all too often I jump into "the heart" of my prayers, seeking God's wisdom with some dilemma I am facing, asking God's intervention in the pains and difficulties of others, and imploring God's reconciling love to bring unity in our broken society. I blow right by adoration. Prayer is the perfect time to adore the God who created this world, and who cares deeply about us. It is the perfect time to express your gratitude.

In essence, we have but two choices. We can be arrogant or we can be grateful. I believe God laughs at our arrogance, even when it breaks his heart. We are nothing without God and we need to be keen to acknowledge it. Frederick Buechner writes, "A Christian is one who is on the way, though not necessarily very far along it, and who has at least some dim and half-baked idea who to thank."[13]

Bible Study

Bible study on the other hand is a bit different. Yes, there is a call to read the scriptures and feel grateful that God stands by us and seeks reconciliation in spite of our never-ending offenses, but it goes well beyond that. It is so very easy to see Bible study as an obligation, to see it as something distasteful that is "good for us," much like eating our spinach and Brussel sprouts (neither of which I care for in the least, I readily admit). Not only does God love us enough to provide us rules for living and to send us his son, he cared enough to work through inspired individuals to chronicle it all in a collection of 66 books to remind us who we are and whose we are. Providing us four accounts of Jesus' life wasn't enough for him. He also gave us the epistles to expound on and clarify Jesus' teachings and example.

When viewed through this lens, Bible study ceases to be an obligation and begins to be a delight. We come to embrace Bible study as the blessing it is. And as I said above, it is more accessible now than ever before in history. We should leap for joy at the opportunities we have for study.

So now we have a foundation for what a disciple is and does. Let's put the action in disciple.

Disciple is, after all, a verb.

STUDY QUESTIONS

What comes to mind as you contemplate the many small ways you share God's love with others?

What can you do to increase your awareness of the opportunities that arise in your daily activities?

Think of a time when you were called on to just listen and be present. How did it impact you?

Envision the changes that would result if you approached all your relationships with the primary intent of meeting their needs. How different would your life be?

Can you identify a time when you prayed for an adversary's good fortune or change of heart?

What does God love? Are your priorities aligned with what God loves?

What situations tempt you to withdraw from your community and go your own way?

Robert McBurnett

CHAPTER 4
Being Discipled

*Blessed is the man who doesn't walk in the
counsel of the wicked,
nor stand on the path of sinners,
nor sit in the seat of scoffers;
but his delight is in Yahweh's law.
On his law he meditates day and night.
He will be like a tree planted by the streams of
water,
that produces its fruit in its season,
whose leaf also does not wither.
Whatever he does shall prosper.*

Psalm 1:1-3

A disciple then, is a follower and a learner committed to developing his character and growing more Christlike.

Roger S. Greenway

Now that we've laid a foundation for understanding discipleship, it is time to put it to work and the first natural step is to examine how you can grow in your faith.

Look about you. Survey the landscape. Then make a list of people who influence you. Not just those who have a daily impact, but think broadly. Don't fear your list will be too long, because it can't be too long. You might use the list you made in Chapter 2 as a launching pad for this exercise if you like. Once you've compiled your list, you then can divide the names into three categories: those you perceive will influence your spiritual growth, those you believe will lead you towards growing worldly success, and third, those that fall somewhere in between.

I created my list on my computer because I am a spreadsheet guy by nature. I put all the names down the left-hand column and then created a column for each category. I then copied each name into the category column where I envision them currently.

"Why use a spreadsheet?" you say. Because as you work through this exercise, names will move from one category to another as you reflect more deeply on the effects these people have on you, and the spreadsheet template allows the flexibility for these changes. If you're not spreadsheet–inclined, get some index cards and put a single name on each card. Resist the urge to write the category on the cards at the outset, because here again you will find that many of them will move from category to category. You can then make a pile for each category and toss each card in the pile that seems most appropriate for that person. Don't agonize over getting them in the right piles, because you will revise and adjust several times as you go.

Be expansive. Make a very long list. Fill up the spreadsheet; fill out lots of cards (really, they're not that expensive). Think beyond natural boundaries. Don't just look at people in your church circles and Bible studies. What you are looking for are the people who have an influence over you and I assure you they are everywhere. They will appear when and where you least expect them. Expand your list as additional names come to you during this process.

I've been asked if the list should be limited to people who are alive. I don't think so, at least for the purpose at hand. We are strongly affected by indelible memories from experiences with those who have preceded us in death. Now I will suggest you not name every historical person from which you draw inspiration. By way of example, I have learned so very much from reading about Abraham Lincoln, but including him on this list would only clutter it up. On the other hand, my paternal grandmother had a huge, direct impact on me that continues even today. She's on my list.

Relax, since there is no right or wrong here. It's your list. You're not going to mail it in for a grade. It won't go on your Permanent Record (for those of you on whom that moniker is lost, those of us of a certain age were constantly threatened in school that all of our misdeeds would go on our Permanent Record and "follow you for the rest of your life"). This is your list and is useful solely for framing your thinking around growing as a disciple of Jesus Christ. Modify it as you wish. And know this, you will modify it over and over, which is to say you don't get only one shot at getting it right.

The purpose here is twofold; first, to build the discipline of being intentional, asking questions such as:
> Where is this person leading me?
> Is this someone who will encourage or impair my spiritual development?
> In what ways can/should they lead me?
> If someone asked me if I were following this person's lead, would I enthusiastically
> reply YES and know why?
> If someone told me I resembled that person, would I take it as a compliment?

Second, the purpose is to raise your awareness of influence. People all around you lead you, whether you acknowledge it or not. Lift up your head, open your eyes, and acknowledge it. Many times I have found myself in a situation I didn't want to be in, only to realize I had followed someone there without any awareness I had followed them, nor where we were headed. How much pain and difficulty could have been avoided if I had only lifted my head, opened my eyes, looked where we were going, and asked these questions?

And don't be deceived by titles. True leadership cannot be conferred. It has to be earned.

I have known people in organizational leadership positions who I wouldn't follow into a burger joint even if I hadn't eaten in three days. Nevertheless, they held positions of leadership and the titles that went with them. I also well remember an acknowledged expert on motivation, who knew all the theory and motivational techniques, but when I met with folks in his organization, I learned his practical misapplication of these principles was a source of jokes and derision among his staff. He only had the outward appearance of being a motivational leader.

Alternatively, some of the most effective and admired leaders I have observed in the workplace were entrenched in the bowels of the organization working hard, laboring effectively, and enriching people's lives. They carried no such titles or designations.

So I now introduce two pairs of terms. The first pair is Spiritual Guides and Worldly Guides. We can, and should, learn from each, but it is essential we distinguish each from the other as we embark on this journey.

The other pair of terms is Indirect Discipling and Direct Discipling. Both means are effective and you should engage in both of them. Although a certain shift in mindset, a shift in focus, may be required. David Augsburger labels it serenity: "Serenity is valuing what you have done in life more than reviewing and defending the record of what you have done; it is prizing what is good and right more than what appears to be good or is praised as right."[14] His concept of serenity captures the nature of what we're after.

Now, let's explore these concepts.

Spiritual Guides

Spiritual Guides are those persons who lead you on Discipleship Road, the ones who live consistently following the teachings and example of Christ. Do not read that to say that they have achieved Christlikeness, rather that they are modeling Christian living.

The first person that comes to mind is a friend I

met through a ministry we share. He radiates kindness and joy in spite of several difficulties in his life, including serious health issues. Tim never sees me that he doesn't stop, inquire about my recent activities, and encourage me to continue ministering to others. Tim loves the Lord and he loves me, and he doesn't hold back from telling me so. Tim is very special to me, and I know I am one of his very best friends. But as I step back and take it all in, I realize Tim treats everyone that way. Everyone is Tim's best friend. He takes a personal interest in each and every person in his life, delivering his own brand of joy and encouragement. Truly, Tim has hundreds of best friends. How Christ-like is that? When I grow up, I want to be Tim.

I have another friend, David. I know David from work. David is kind, committed, and extremely competent in his job, a very demanding one. He hits the door running every day and doesn't slow down until he heads home at its conclusion. Yet, his family remains his first priority. He is ever focused on the development of character in his children and he sets a very high example for them. David never talks about his faith or the Bible at work, instead he just lives them out! No matter what crushing deadline he is facing, he is always the first to volunteer to help on a project or to bail out others who are falling behind. He makes time to lend a compassionate ear when troubles hit any of us. He would never admit it because he doesn't see it, but God's grace flows through him like a mighty river. David has cultivated Paul's fruit of the spirit. When I grow up, I want David's aura to abide in me.

Terry is a pastor, and he's also a great preacher. I've come to understand that not all great preachers are great at pastoring and not all great pastors are great at preaching. Terry is outstanding at both. In spite of the many demands on Terry's schedule, he makes time for his friends as well as for his congregants. When there is pain, Terry is there, and when he is there, he is there. He doesn't check his watch or his phone, thinking about what comes next on his schedule. He is fully focused on the person in front of him, truly engaged in their situation.

When he preaches, he brings massive comprehension of Jesus and the Bible, yet at the same time he is ever so human, never shying away from sharing his vulnerabilities and weaknesses. He delivers great Biblical wisdom to me. He nurtures my growth. He picks me up when I stumble. He is so far ahead of me on the spiritual road, but never so distant that he doesn't look over his shoulder to make sure I am still following. When I grow up, I want to lead people to Christ and shepherd them along The Way like Terry.

I'm also thinking about my friend Martha. Long

ago, Martha and I were peers and worked together on a mutual business project that came around once a year. Since then, our paths have diverged, but we still check in from time to time. Even with long breaks between check-ins, we always pick up the conversation right where we left off.

Martha has gone on to a very responsible executive position with an incredibly important not-for-profit organization. Her organization highly values her for her contribution and acknowledges that many of their achievements are attributable to her. She continues to be a great source of professional wisdom for me. She has matured into that rare combination of being a tough, serious, hardnosed, seasoned, senior executive (essential for any successful organizational leader) while being fun, caring, and compassionate (essential for what God created us to be). When I grow up, I want to be decisive, authoritative, and, at the same time, fun and compassionate like Martha.

A certain public person, one whom I won't give a name here, is known far and wide for leadership. The list of organizations he has led boggles the mind. For most men or women, having the opportunity to lead any one of these groups would be the pinnacle of a lifelong career. He has always led from his convictions and, while he will apologize for his actions or decisions when he believes it is warranted, he never apologizes for who he is or for what he stands. He can mingle with the highest of the high, then turn and deal tenderly with the commonest of the common. While I have only met him in passing on a couple of occasions, I have followed his life and legacy from a distance. I decided years ago, I wanted to be a man of character modeled after him. More significantly, I was struck by the adoration for him from his family.

Most leaders who have risen to great professional achievements have done so at great expense to their families. One only has to watch this man around his wife and children to see that he has true, genuine relationships with each one of them that can only be the result of time invested with them. Years ago he was asked to contemplate all his accomplishments and to choose the one he was most proud of. His response was, "The fact that our children still come home." I decided right then and there that if there was one achievement to strive for it was this. When I grow up, I want to have served well and loved well like him.

I need to close out this section and can't do so without confessing I have left out the single most influential Spiritual Guide in my life. I can't give her a pseudonym or hide any facts here. I also can't even scratch the surface of how she guides me and encourages me all day, every day. That is my wife, without peer the most Christ-like person I have ever met.

Her spiritual gifts are numbered like the sands on the beach. She radiates God's love, compassion, and grace wherever she goes. When I grow up, I want to still follow in her footsteps daily.

These are all people who lead in spiritual ways, even though I doubt they wake up thinking, "I'm going to lead people to Christ today." Nevertheless, they are Spiritual Guides for me.

Worldly Guides

Worldly Guides lead us in ways that lead to success. Previously I said God doesn't call us to be successful, he calls us to be faithful; however, do not misconstrue that to mean that success is irrelevant. We all want to be successful. We just have differing definitions of what it means to be successful. We can learn very valuable lessons from these Worldly Guides who navigate well the challenges of life. Similar to Spiritual Guides, we learn valuable life lessons from them, but we also need to be aware and deliberate about what aspects we choose to emulate and where their lessons are leading us.

I spoke above about the expert on motivation that fell short in the eyes of his staff. He most definitely possessed a wealth of wisdom on motivation, and I learned so very much from him about effective motivation and how impactful it can be, as he was extremely wise with much to share. I took advantage of many opportunities to study and learn from him.

I also came to realize that with some people their actions and beliefs don't always match. An incredibly helpful lesson to carry as I grew and matured, it also causes me to stop and account for my actions from time to time and to assess them through the lens of my beliefs. Many times, upon reflection, I detected a significant mismatch. Following guides such as these can lead to much worldly success and a measured and a tempered application of what is shared greatly benefits me.

I once observed Luis, who was working his way up the management ladder. He was successful running a segment of our business and was elevated to a larger segment of the business and then one even larger. Luis was a young, rising star in the company, and was exalted for his communication skills. I learned a lot from him about how to deliver both good and bad news in a positive manner. He was masterful at surveying the landscape and determining how best to deploy resources (fiscal, physical, and human) in order to achieve his objectives and for those in his charge.

I also saw how devastating his victories could be for the other component parts of the company. So very often, his segment's gain was at the expense of other segments of the company. At times, his victories left others stripped of their dignity. As he rose to lead larger groups, he found some of those victimized segments reporting to him. At best, the people he shorted in the past were distrustful of his leadership. His positive messages were now regarded with suspicion and skepticism.

Achieving the very best advantage for you and yours often leads to great advancement, but when you grab all you can for you and yours at the expense of others, the whole is often worse off for it. I learned to lead while being vigilant for opportunities to advance everyone in the process. Above all, I learned to leave every person's dignity intact at all costs. I decided that a big part of victory lies in learning to win by extending grace to others and that personal dignity is inviolate.

I'll bring in yet another public figure I know. This man's wealth and possessions are considerable, and a large swath of Americans would aspire to any of his several positions and accomplishments. His basic philosophy is "grab all you can." In business deals, he wrings every advantage out of every deal, leaving no dollar on the table. He is constantly on alert for the next big deal. His worldly gains are enviable, to say the least. The fruits of his labors are not all sweet, however. His winner-take-all drive means that most people never come back for a second deal. Many are left with nothing with which to deal and others find the process so distasteful, they have no interest in a return engagement. His skill at manipulating a deal leaves him widely distrusted.

What did I learn from this successful businessman? I learned that he who wins doesn't always win.

Donald is a friend I know from church circles. He is a very successful salesman. Two of the keys to his success are his engaging, sincere personality and his willingness to go where the customers are. Going where the customers are entails a lot of travel – a lot of travel. Donald's family remains very important to him and he carefully guards the sanctity of weekends, committing Sundays to regular church attendance and Saturdays and Sundays to activities with his wife and children. He has succeeded in most aspects the world values: influence, prestige, and money. He amasses frequent flyer miles at a dizzying pace. As a result, he and his family take trips to places I can only dream of… when he can clear the time to go, that is. Finances never stand in the way of opportunities for his kids. I admire his career success. I respect how he guards time for his family on the weekends.

On the other hand, he isn't there for them during the week—missing out on many of their great victories and celebrations and being separated at times when they needed healing and comfort. I have learned a lot of valuable lessons from Donald, but have chosen not to follow his lead comprehensively.

(Now for another bit of my story. Midcareer I had what some would call a professional setback, a career redirection. In plain English, I got fired. I had several career successes to build on and I was assessing my options. A friend met with me and said I had all the attributes to be a very successful consultant. I told him that sounded intriguing, but I was committed to not being on the road constantly, citing the unfairness it would impose on my family.

He said he had the same reservation, but then realized that the hours he had been working prior to becoming a consultant were such that he was never home anyway. "I might as well have been on the road for all the time I spent at the office," he said.

In that moment, I knew I was this friend. Yes, I managed my church commitments, coached our youth athletic teams and never missed a game, play or awards ceremony. I also knew I never saw my kids off to school; I had been at the office long before they ever got up. I rarely made it home in time for dinner and honestly couldn't recall a time I helped with homework. No, I wasn't on the road like my friend Donald, but I sure was following his life-/

career-pattern in many ways.)

I once had the privilege of working with Brittany. Brittany was one of the smartest people I have ever known, and I have known a lot of incredibly smart people. She was driven to make the world a better place. She was a fabulous mother and mentor. Brittany was the epitome of constant improvement. She had an incredible drive to win, to be the best at everything, but we could always do it better next time.

While her abilities and commitment drove us to great achievements, she came across as incredibly intimidating. I can't remember a time when she wasn't the smartest person in the room. No one would challenge or question her. I learned that true success comes when you achieve your objectives, still realize you are the smartest person in the room, yet no one else leaves feeling that way.

All of these people have had great worldly success and I learned valuable traits from each of them. But if I follow them intensely, I will end up with worldly gains at the expense of my spiritual growth. They are representative of my Worldly Guides.

The In-Betweens

Right now, I imagine you're thinking of the people on your list and re-sorting them into the categories above. Some who come to mind are clearly Spiritual Guides and some are Worldly Guides, but my guess is the vast majority of the people on your list fit snuggly in neither category. And that is as it should be.

It isn't necessary, or intended, for everyone in your life to shepherd you somewhere. Most of the people in your life are there to enhance your life, leading you neither here nor there. You can simply enjoy them and experience life alongside them. Don't expend a lot of energy trying to fit everyone into the Spiritual Guide or Worldly Guide columns. Actually, some of them are in your life so you can be a Spiritual Guide for them. Much more about that later, though.

What you should reflect on from time to time is whether someone in this In Betweens category needs to be evaluated more carefully and moved into one of the others.

The Movers

The real value in this exercise comes with a fourth

group: the Movers. Movers are those who move from category to category. If you set your list finalizing it once and for all where no one moves from your original assessment, you have missed the point. The key here is to increase your awareness as you develop and grow. People change, as you surely will. What you value will also change. New revelations about yourself and others will come. You must be willing to take a second, third, and tenth look at those who have influence over you. You don't need a column (or pile if you are working in index card-mode) for The Movers. They will be slotted in the appropriate column of the three above, and just moved around from time to time.

* * * * *

And that is a wonderful place to start these considerations. Christy, my wife, is forever telling me, "You're becoming just like Mary," or "Do you realize when you are around Bill, you begin to talk like him?"

The answer in these situations is invariably "No" except when it is a defiant, "I do not!" Which, of course, prompts her to prove that I actually do. These situations invariably reveal that these people influence me in ways of which I am unaware, in which case I am at great risk of following them unintentionally. You need to be intentional in determining whom you will follow, and in which column you categorize them.

Periodically, you need to pull out your list and run through it again. As you do, you will read most names and move on along. Others will give you cause to pause. When this happens, stop and focus on that person and your current relationship with them. How much influence are they having on you right now? Are you following them unintentionally? Should you be following them in some aspect of your life? Should they be in your Spiritual Guides list or on you Worldly Guides list? If so, how will this shift alter your actions?

Don't let the folks on your Spiritual and Worldly Guides list remain static, either. Circumstances change, people change, and new revelations come to light. These should all evoke reassessment and possibly a change of relational status. Let me share a few examples in my life.

I recall a very talented ballplayer from my time in baseball. He immediately contributed on the field and quickly became a fan favorite and media darling. He said all the right things, supported numerous charitable causes, and was forever talking about helping others.

As time passed, it became apparent to his teammates and me that it was all a façade. He had carefully crafted an image for himself with the assistance of a capable public relations team. In the clubhouse, he was surly to the clubhouse attendants and dismissive of his teammates. He quickly moved from the Spiritual Guides list to my Worldly Guides list. From him, I learned the value of being consistent in my personal and public lives.

Before you say, "I knew it. All professional athletes are out for personal gain and only reach out the community as a hollow gesture!" let me share about another ballplayer. He too was very talented and immediately contributed to our on-field success, and was also a fan favorite and media darling. He too said all the right things, was involved with numerous charitable causes, about most of which the public was unknowing.

As time passed, it became apparent he was the same person publicly and personally. He was forever reaching out to the clubhouse staff making sure they were taken care of and treated well. He took a personal interest in the wellbeing of his teammates. He was a man of true character. He moved from my In Betweens list onto my Spiritual Guides list. I learned from him to be consistent in my personal and public lives, and to treat with grace and dignity at all times those who are tasked with meeting my needs.

One of the most frequent questions I get is, "What are professional athletes really like?" I used to struggle with answering the question since they are such a diverse set of individuals, until I realized that is precisely the answer.

Professional athletes are like any other group of people you know, whether it's your co-workers, a church small group, or in a social circle. Some are amazing, beautiful people. Some are real jerks. Some are just schlepping along. Whether the group tilts in one direction or another is irrespective of the setting. Some of the most jerk-infested groups I've encountered have been church-based. Some of the most beatifically minded groups have been social. It is my assessment, however, when it comes to the athletes I encountered, the beautiful people far outnumbered the jerks.

While I'm highlighting people in the public spotlight, let me share one more. This is a highly respected person, very successful in the world of sports. He was not outspoken or loud, but he had a definite aura. He was highly regarded for his staunch adherence to his Christian principles. Through an unexpected turn of events, I learned that he was an investor in the company I happened to work for at the time, which was operating in ways I found unethical (this was early in my career, long before my time in professional sports management). Had I had a Spiritual and Worldly Guides list, I would have immediately moved this public figure from the Spiritual Guides column to my Worldly Guides column, and I wasn't bashful about sharing my disdain for this highly respected public figure with others.

Now, I will also tell you that my in-laws held this person in the highest regard, and we exchanged very harsh words on the matter. Years later, I learned more and more about the man and came to the realization that this was one of his many passive investments and he probably had no insight whatsoever as to how we conducted business. I slot him in my In Betweens column, but in the Highly Admired subcategory. Lesson learned under the heading of Rush to Judgment.

Now for chapter 2 of that story. I had judged the sports figure to be a hypocrite for holding himself out as a paragon of virtue while being in business with a business lacking ethically. It didn't occur to me until years later that, while he had a passive interest in the business, I was working directly for the company and furthering its unethical business practices. Which of us, I ask you, was the guilty one here?

I also remember a very personal relationship that packed a powerful lesson. Jim is an extremely successful professional in our community. He loves his wife, his daughter, and his church beyond measure. When I was a very young man just starting out in business, I knew I wanted what Jim had.

One Sunday during our church's financial pledge campaign, Jim shared his giving experience from the pulpit. He talked about the joys of giving and how his life changed when he began tithing. I was moved and began thinking how I should move in that direction. I was on the Finance Committee for the church, and I was on the team that sorted and recorded the pledge cards when they came in. Imagine how my heart sank when I opened Jim's card only to find a very meager pledge. How could he give that stirring testimony and submit such a paltry commitment? He rocketed onto the Worldly Guides column from the Spiritual Guides list.

I was crushed, not so much by the limits of his financial commitment, but from his deception of the congregation. Now as you might imagine, the work of recording the pledges was highly confidential. I didn't share anything about it even with my wife, but this situation would not leave me alone. I finally went to the pastor, who was also a good friend, and confided my torment. I didn't share any details, just that the pledge so conflicted with Jim's stirring testimony.

My friend gently explained to me that Jim's earnings varied wildly from year to year based on the volume of work generated. He shared that shortly after Jim joined the church, he came to him and said he didn't want to pledge on his estimated earnings and then have the church in a crunch in a year where he didn't earn what he had expected. He told the pastor he would pledge annually on what he was absolutely sure of earning (not very much), but as the year progressed the pastor was to come to him with any special needs and he would meet them to the extent he could at the time.

My friend said, "Remember when we had the electrical problem with the lights in the parking lot? I went to Jim and he wrote a $20,000 check on the spot. Remember when the youth mission trip was saved at the last minute when funds came in? That was Jim. Jim is our backstop. He has never turned me down on a request."

So I ask you, how quickly do you think Jim boomeranged back onto my Spiritual Guides list?

Now, that we have explored the three categories of guides, let's look at the two ways of being discipled.

Indirect Discipling

Indirect Discipling is a very effective and

common means of being discipled. In these situations, the person who is discipling you is likely unaware they are doing so. In many cases, you might never even meet them. Think back to the public figures examples above. Of all the public figures I cited above, I only knew two of them personally and had the privilege of meeting one of the others ever so briefly. I doubt any of them had any idea they were guiding me. The secular world has a name for these guides: role models.

I caution you to be careful in picking who will disciple you indirectly. The default is to admire someone and begin patterning your life after theirs subconsciously. Over time, I have learned to notice when I am being influenced by somebody and to assess what I am learning from them. Most of the time, I make no mention of it to them. I just watch their behavior and demeanor and take notes. These are indirect discipling experiences.

Clearly, this is the case with public figures I've never met and often with many of the folks I know personally (as well as those on my list who are deceased, of course). The public figure above with the huge professional accomplishments and the great family relationships would be a prime example. Although I met him later in life, I never imagined I would ever run into him, let alone meet him. Rather, I just read what I could about him and paid attention to events where he caught the media's attention. I was being discipled by him from afar, and that didn't change after our couple of passing encounters.

I have taken pleasure from similar experiences with people I know, even some close to me. I identify them as someone whose actions merit emulation. I seek opportunities to be with them and pay close attention to their actions and how they treat others. It should come as no surprise to you that people I choose as models are people I truly enjoy being around.

In part though, it comes down to intentionality on my part. I take notice of them when I am in their presence and reflect on it when I am away from them. This process allows me to distill what it is that makes them special, seeking insight into how and why they succeed. It is nearly impossible to pattern yourself after another without isolating the behaviors that make them worth following.

Let me share my experience with a particular individual who has had an extreme impact on my life. It well illustrates at least two key lessons about being discipled.

I first encountered Chris at a training day for Certified Public Accountants. As a CPA, I am required to get certain hours of training each year under an umbrella known as continuing professional education. Chris was the presenter for one of the sessions I chose that day. He was dynamic with a compelling message to share: exciting, excitable, right on into inspiring. Now, I will be the first to admit that dynamic, exciting, and inspiring are not attributes generally associated with CPAs, even for those who lead training sessions, but Chris was truly the exception.

The next time a training day like this was posted, I noticed he was presenting once again and I made sure to attend his session. It was on a very different topic, but the result was the same—dynamic, with a compelling message to share—exciting, excitable, right on into inspiring. I fell into the habit of searching each training day notice to see if he was presenting to ensure I was in the room on those occasions when he was. He was gaining quite a following. That first day, there were probably 50 of us in the room. Within a couple of years, he was drawing 200-300 to his sessions, and you learned to arrive early if you wanted a seat.

Chris led me indirectly in ways you can only imagine. I dedicated a binder to his presentations that I kept in my study. I filed the outline for each of his presentations along with my notes in it. Each section was tabbed by subject and date attended. I referenced them constantly. At one point, I was so inspired by one of his presentations, I used it as the platform for a six-week study I presented in my Sunday school class.

I don't know how many of these sessions I had attended, at least six, when I left one saying to myself, "I just gotta meet this guy!" Now, this was pretty presumptuous. I mean, I was one of hundreds in the crowd. I also knew he ran a very successful business and had clearly devoted considerable time to prepare and present these training sessions. All that, plus he had a family he loved dearly who provided many of the illustrations in his presentations. I convinced myself he was just out of my reach, but, oh man, if only…

The thought kept gnawing at me until one day I picked up the phone with great trepidation and called the number he listed on all his outlines. (Not only did he run a very successful business, the business bore his name.) I shook as the phone rang on the other end, all the while trying to assure myself that when I couldn't get through to the great man nothing had been lost because he didn't know me from the Man in the Moon, and I could continue to hide anonymously in future sessions undetected. Well, my heart really began racing when the receptionist said, "Sure, let me put you through."

The next voice I heard was Chris'. I stuttered that

I had attended many of his CPA presentations and considered myself a Disciple of Chris. I said I would love to meet him face to face and asked if we could meet for lunch one day (one of my bosses once said, "Everyone likes to eat," and extending a meal invitation has actually proven highly effective for me). He had his calendar in front of him and offered an opportunity two days away. Needless to say, I quickly accepted lest he have second thoughts.

Here is the first lesson in the story: Ask! As another boss of mine taught me, "You never get a 'Yes' if you don't ask the question." You will be shocked at how many very busy, influential people will make time to sit and converse with you if you merely gird your loins and ask.

So, we met for lunch (we both had grilled chicken salad), and as soon as we sat down, I began gushing all over him—how much I had gained from his teaching, how I put it into practice, what I experienced as a result, even sharing that I turned one of his sessions into a Sunday school series. I distinctly remember saying at the outset, "I owe you some royalties, because I have been using your material liberally."

I also remember his response, "You owe me nothing. It's all in the public domain. All my sessions are right out of the Bible."

He almost had to pick me up off the floor. No way did he have CPAs lining up to hear him teach the Bible, but sure enough that was the case. They had no idea he was spreading the keys to the life Christ taught us. Just to make sure I knew he wasn't fooling around, he listed off three or four of the sessions I had attended, calling each by name: this one is straight out of Ezekiel, this one from Isaiah, that one from Matthew.

During the lunch, he called me out for a spiritual gift I a) didn't realize I had, and b) didn't even realize was a spiritual gift. He said, "It's in Romans somewhere I think. Not entirely sure, but I think it's there."

In hindsight, I know he knew it was in Romans; it was his way of baiting me into reading Romans, and of course it worked. I have employed this technique with others many times since.

As we parted company, he asked to continue the conversation over lunch again one day soon. I don't have to tell you I readily accepted.

Now, I will forewarn you the extension of the conversation is unusual in situations like this, but make the call and at least benefit from having the initial conversation. You have no idea how it might expand your horizons and thinking. Here is the second lesson to take from this story: not only did he solidify his place on my Spiritual Guides list, but he also became one of my go-to mentors. He became a valued mentor, which brings us to...

Direct Discipling

Direct Discipling is where the magic happens. Once you identify a Spiritual Guide and get to know them, you can move into the active phase of discipling: Direct Discipling. In this forum, they actively disciple you by phone or in person. Maybe you tell them you are looking to them to lead you in discipleship, maybe you don't, but you're clear about building a relationship.

Many of my Spiritual Guides would never acknowledge they are discipling me, actually most of them would deny it. They don't see themselves as worthy of discipling someone else. These folks generally see themselves as just another pilgrim on the road to being better Christians. They will quickly tell you they are just making it along and are not worthy of being followed. At best, they might admit to being on the journey alongside me.

Typically, the people who Directly Disciple me come through some connection from work, personal interests, social engagements, or occasionally through a church dynamic. Our conversations and meetings thrive on that connection, but the conversations quickly expand into other areas of our lives, which inevitably route through our faiths. These are the people to whom I look to grow my faith. Sometimes we talk overtly about faith, but often it can also be a relationship where we learn from each other's experiences.

The most fruitful discipling experiences, however, flower from a depth of understanding rooted in sharing our faith experiences. Tim, David, Terry, and Martha all fall into this category. With the exception of Terry, none of them started out on a faith base, but they have evolved there over time. With David it happened very, very quickly; Tim took a little longer; and Martha got there over a period of years.

In all cases, something attracted me to them, which I would characterize as their exhibiting a caring disposition towards the people around them. They were people I just wanted to know better. In very few cases did I set out with a Direct Discipleship relationship in mind. The key is at some point I realized I could learn a lot from them and I became intentional about probing what they had to share with me and took it to heart. I so look forward to each opportunity to learn from each of them.

Yet another interesting aspect of these Direct

Discipling people is that with many of them, I can touch off a pretty lively debate by telling them they are discipling me. Most of them would quickly counter that they are the disciple and I am the one discipling them. In truth, we are discipling each other. We both grow through the relationship.

The scriptural reference that comes to mind is Ecclesiastes 4:9-12:

Two are better than one, because they have a good reward for their labor. For if they fall, the one will lift up his fellow; but woe to him who is alone when he falls, and doesn't have another to lift him up. Again, if two lie together, then they have warmth; but how can one keep warm alone? If a man prevails against one who is alone, two shall withstand him; and a threefold cord is not quickly broken.

And make no mistake, the third strand is the Holy Spirit.

More significantly, I am learning from them all the time—especially when we are apart—as I work to engrain those lessons into my daily life. It is amazing how when I find myself in a tight spot, or not knowing which way to go with a decision, one of them will come to mind. I find myself thinking, "What would my friend Martha do?" It's not exactly "What would Jesus do?" but it is pretty close.

The other dimension is when I am bearing down on some decision or project and hear that little, irritating voice say, "You know, Tim would never do that." I am stopped in my tracks, because frustrating as the little voice is, it is almost never ever wrong, and the real message is, "If Tim would never do that, and you know he wouldn't, why are you even thinking about doing it?"

Direct Discipling is without a doubt the most effective means of growing your faith, but make no mistake, Indirect Discipling is also highly effective. Be intentional in employing both means to become the person you were designed to be.

Now that we have examined how we are discipled, let's move to the next stage–discipling others.

I reiterate – Disciple is a verb.

STUDY QUESTIONS

How difficult did you find separating Spiritual Guides from Worldly Guides?

Did you identify more Spiritual Guides or Worldly Guides?

Did you find the concept of intentionally assessing where each of your Guides is leading you to be new?

Do you now feel emboldened to approach people you admire for advice and counsel? To invite them to disciple you in the Direct Discipleship manner?

Robert McBurnett

CHAPTER 5
Discipling Others

We always give thanks to God for all of you, mentioning you in our prayers, remembering without ceasing your work of faith and labor of love and patience of hope in our Lord Jesus Christ, before our God and Father. We know, brothers loved by God, that you are chosen, and that our Good News came to you not in word only, but also in power, and in the Holy Spirit, and with much assurance. You know what kind of men we showed ourselves to be among you for your sake. You became imitators of us, and of the Lord, having received the word in much affliction, with joy of the Holy Spirit, so that you became an example to all who believe in Macedonia and in Achaia. For from you the word of the Lord has been declared, not only in Macedonia and Achaia, but also in every place your faith toward God has gone out; so that we need not to say anything.

1 Thessalonians 1:2-8

If you want to lift up yourself, lift up someone else.

Roger S. Greenway

Let's revisit Zechariah 8:23 again:

Yahweh of Armies says: "In those days, ten men will take hold, out of all the languages of the nations, they will take hold of the skirt of him who is a Jew, saying, 'We will go with you, for we have heard that God is with you.'"

Our immediate inclination is to see ourselves as one of the ten people attached to the robe (skirt) of the Jew, and we have now considered ways to attach ourselves to worthy guides. Now let's turn our attention to the real work.

We need to turn the passage around and see ourselves as the Jew, the one whose robe others seek to grab. This does not come naturally for most of us, but we must engage in this critical work. And not just some of us, but all of us. It is your calling and it is your duty, a duty that when done right becomes the source of deep, enduring joy and fulfillment. Yes, God pours his grace into our lives to bring us joy and fulfillment, but the real reason he pours his grace into us is so we will in turn pour it into the lives of others. This is an incredibly daunting assignment, but we are not left on our own to accomplish it, because God promises to be with us every step of the way.

Throughout the Bible, God assures us he will stand with us. God said to Jacob, *Behold, I am with you, and will keep you, wherever you go, and will bring you again into this land. For I will not leave you, until I have done that which I have spoken of to you.* (Genesis 28:15); the Lord told Joshua, *No man will be able to stand before you all the days of your life. As I was with Moses, so I will be with you. I will not fail you nor forsake you. Be strong and courageous; for you shall cause this people to inherit the land which I swore to their fathers to give them.* (Joshua 1:5-6); and most significantly, Jesus left his disciples with these final words, *Behold, I am with you always, even to the end of the age.* (Matthew 28:20).

Yes, God will be with you.

Our call then is to live in the presence of God, to be his ambassadors, exemplifying a life lived with Jesus. We are invited to live a life with Christ, a life lived in his presence, while aspiring to live a fully Christ-like life.

When you commit to living that life, the world around you takes notice and the people you encounter will want what you have. Maybe it is not an intentional decision they make, but they will see evidence of the fruit of the spirit: love, joy, peace, patience, kindness, goodness, and the others. True, we draw inner strength from the fruit of the spirit, but when fully in bloom, the fruit inevitably radiates. When you begin living out the fruit, you radiate the love of Christ in ways both large and small. This is when the "ten men from other nations" will reach for the hem of your robe.

In a manner similar to the assessment you made in the last chapter about those who influence you, let's see who is attached to your robe, and identify others who should be. Once again, this is an area where you need to be attentive and intentional. It's not enough to focus on those who seek you out; you are called to be mindful of all on whom you can have a kingdom-building influence.

Now, the natural tendency at this point is to say, "Well, I'm not called to be a leader. I just need to concentrate on growing in my faith," but it doesn't work that way. Taking your place to lead others is the spiritual equivalent of our perpetuating the species.

Remember, God said to Noah, *Be fruitful and*

increase in number and fill the earth. And he promised Abram, *Then I will make my covenant between me and you and will greatly increase your numbers. As for me, this is my covenant with you: You will be the father of many nations. No longer will you be called Abram; your name will be Abraham, for I have made you a father of many nations. I will make you very fruitful. I will make nations of you.* Abram/Abraham was destined to give birth to a family that would in turn propagate a faith.

Similarly, Jesus set the example for us when he called his disciples. Revisit John 1 with me.

One of the two who heard John, and followed him, was Andrew, Simon Peter's brother. He first found his own brother, Simon, and said to him, "We have found the Messiah!" (which is, being interpreted, Christ). He brought him to Jesus. Jesus looked at him, and said, "You are Simon the son of Jonah. You shall be called Cephas" (which is by interpretation, Peter). On the next day, he was determined to go out into Galilee, and he found Philip. Jesus said to him, "Follow me." Now Philip was from Bethsaida, of the city of Andrew and Peter. Philip found Nathanael, and said to him, "We have found him, of whom Moses in the law, and the prophets, wrote: Jesus of Nazareth, the son of Joseph."

Nathanael said to him, "Can any good thing come

out of Nazareth?"

Philip said to him, "Come and see."

When Jesus saw Nathanael approaching, he said of him, "Here truly is an Israelite in whom there is no deceit." "How do you know me?" Nathanael asked. Jesus answered, "I saw you while you were still under the fig tree before Philip called you." Then Nathanael declared, "Rabbi, you are the Son of God; you are the king of Israel." Jesus said, "You believe because I told you I saw you under the fig tree. You will see greater things than that." He then added, "Very truly I tell you, you will see 'heaven open, and the angels of God ascending and descending on' the Son of Man."

This is the pattern John provides us: one person bringing another, and that person bringing one more. One-to-one-to-one. Yes, Peter speaks at Pentecost and 3,000 come to the faith, but the proscribed method is one-to-one-to-one, on and on.

My challenge to you is, "What are you doing to keep the chain going?"

I want to pause here to highlight an additional precept. While we are to encourage and provide guidance to those who are on the path alongside us, it is not our job to convert people into a life in Christ. We are to model Christ's life for them in an enticing manner and to be ready to share our experiences with them. It is Jesus' job, and Jesus' alone, to convert them.

I also firmly believe we are called to nurture them, not to clean them up. Christ will work in their lives for those purposes. You are called to work on your own reclamation while encouraging them in their efforts. We need to remember Jesus' charge, "Why do you look at the speck of sawdust in your brother's eye and pay no attention to the plank in your own eye?" However, should they ask for help, by all means help them. Nurture, encourage, lead!

The first critical step here is to advance your self-awareness of how you live your faith, and the fruit of the spirit is an excellent gauge.

(Let me pause here highlighting this fruit of the spirit. By way of reminder, Paul wrote, *But the fruit of the Spirit is love, joy, peace, patience, kindness, goodness, faith, gentleness, and self-control.* (Galatians 5:22-23a). I draw your attention the word fruit. Paul writes about fruit, not fruits. Note also the verb: fruit is.

For Paul, these are not individual fruits, but rather they combine to comprise the fruit of the spirit. I have heard many sermons and lessons on these "fruits" and when I came to the understanding that it is the combination of traits that are manifested in the fruit of the spirit, it took on new significance as I realized I had to cultivate them all in concert. So, when you read on and find I insist on referring to fruit of the spirit in singular form, you will know it was quite intentional.)

Now let's examine the fruit in your life. Is your natural tendency to greet people in love and kindness? Do you exude an air of joy? If I ask your colleagues if you're a good person, how will they respond? Is there a peace about you? How's that patience thing working for you? Are you gentle and under control? And in the end, faithfulness might be the most important and the most difficult of them all to assess.

The only way you are going to grow in these ways is to be intentional about growing all nine dimensions. No, they won't grow at the same pace, creating perfect symmetry. Yes, they will manifest themselves in your life as you grow in discipleship, but a true disciple stops at regular intervals to assess where s/he stands with each.

I recently told one of my Spiritual Guides, "I've lost my joy. I can't explain it. I don't know where I lost it, I just know I've lost it."

We began exploring and realized I had allowed

outside influences (reversals in the workplace primarily) to push the joy out of my life. I had become so intense about persevering through a particularly stressful period, it overtook me. Not only was I drained of joy, but I was also lacking in patience, kindness and self-control. Peace and gentleness were completely out of the question. Once he helped me come to this realization, I implemented an immediate course correction.

The more time I spent with it, the more it became increasingly evident the root cause was deviation in my faithfulness. I still read and studied and prayed every day, but I wasn't letting it soak into my being. It had little to no impact on how I went through my day. I had attempted to push through on my own merit and efforts.

It was time to confront the log in my own eye. I could not effectively disciple others (many of whom were counting on me to do so) in that condition. And through this evaluative process, I realized just how much joy I derive from discipling others.

Let me be really clear here. Do not wait until you get the fruit of the spirit overflowing in your life to engage in discipling others. Just as I said above that we are to nurture others, not clean them up, so it is with ourselves. You work on your own weaknesses in tandem with nurturing others.

Similar to the exercise in Being Discipled, we'll now take an inventory of the people in your life that you can disciple. Unlike the lists you developed in Being Discipled, there is no worldly/spiritual contrast. The distinction here is in how you approach this work.

Make a list. Please, please make a list. Don't just say to yourself, "Oh, I've got this." Set some time aside with as few distractions as you can. Think it through thoroughly. The objective is to address one fundamental question: Who is in my path?

The list of people you can influence is endless; however, the list of folks you can disciple is much shorter. These are people on whom you can have a direct impact. There are dozens right under your nose, many of whom you do not even notice. They yearn for you to teach them, and you are completely unaware of it. The categories you want to isolate are:

> Disciples - those you intentionally disciple/mentor in some fashion.
> Followers - those whom you perceive might follow your example (if you probe deeply here, you should be able to surface some names of people you didn't realize you are influencing).
> Overlooked – those standing right before you in your day-to-day who would benefit from your influence.

Questions you should contemplate as you assess your discipling of them might include:

Disciples

Do I lead in ways directly influenced by my Christian faith? (Whether you are teaching them the faith, or directly using faith-based examples are two entirely different questions.)

Am I assessing their progress not only in terms of increased productivity and success, but also on the basis of their growing in Christ-likeness?

Is nurturing them one of my very highest priorities or am I doing it out of obligation? (If the answer is "out of obligation," I suggest your reevaluate the relationship.)

Followers

Who seems stuck on the path and needs to assess where it leads next?

Who is showing signs that they want to be discipled – in a specific way or in general?

Who dwells on personal advancement and acquisition at the expense of others? How receptive might they be to changing?

Who turns to me with questions and repeatedly seeks my advice?

How can I be more intentional in guiding them? (This is not the same question as whether you are directly coaching them, more on that later.)

Overlookeds

Who do I know that is starting out on their faith journey?

Who is looking for purpose in their life and has yet to find direction?

Who do I know that consistently tries to do the right thing, but lacks confidence?

How can/should I reach out to them?

The tendency here is to begin eliminating people from the list, but your challenge is to widen, not narrow, the field. There are so many ways to say, "Oh that person doesn't count because . . ."

One assessment that needs to be quickly cast

aside is age – "I can't possibly disciple someone older than I am." Au contraire! I well remember a spiritual retreat I was on years ago. One of my very close compatriots said proudly, "My sixteen year-old son is my spiritual role model." He had amazing admiration for his son's faith and he wanted what his son had. Clearly, the younger was discipling the older.

Escape hatches to avoid in making your list:

> S/he's older than I am.

> S/he has been on the faith path for years, and I am new to the faith.

> S/he isn't interested in a spiritual journey.

> We are in a secular relationship and introducing the spiritual dimension will just complicate matters.

> Who am I to interfere in their personal lives?

> If I introduce them to Christ, it will change our relationship.

I'm going to stop here one more time and beg you – MAKE A LIST! If you want to read on and get the full spectrum of the concept, then fine, but make an unbreakable commitment to yourself that you will sit down and MAKE A LIST! Their futures hang in the balance–please do not leave them dangling. Christ is counting on you.

When you get tired and when the pressures of the world are closing in, you will be tempted to deemphasize your discipling work. When those times come as they surely will, I implore you to ask yourself, "Why would I deprive her/him of the joy of knowing Christ?"

Now let's turn our attention to how we disciple and again I will offer two paths – Direct and Indirect (no bonus points for creativity there).

Direct Discipling

Direct Discipling is where your list comes squarely into play. We'll walk briefly through some steps here, but in Direct Discipling you take a role actively working in their lives.

Look at your list of folks who are in your path to lead along their faith journeys. Scan your list for those who you believe will willingly invite your influence, surely there will be several. Much as you did with your Spiritual and Worldly Guides list, make two columns and identify two categories—those who you think might be interested in your direct guidance and those who are not. When you are in doubt,

I suggest you put them in the Direct Discipling column for now. (Index cards will work here, too.)

Next, go back and look at your list and reflect on each person. Focus on who s/he is and how you are involved in her/his life. See each as the whole person they are, acknowledging that while you can indeed lead a group of people in discipleship, you can only disciple people as individuals.

Years ago, I attended a daylong class to earn a license in order to coach my son's soccer team. The instructor was a man whose wisdom extended far beyond coaching soccer. At one point, he said, "What is the most effective means of coaching your team?"

Hands shot up and many of the high-achievers offered their ideas. He rejected each of them diplomatically as he moved from aspiring coach to aspiring coach. He let the group exhaust itself, at which point he wisely observed, "You cannot coach a team, you can only coach individual players. You can design drills and games to improve the team's skills, but when it comes to actual coaching, you can only coach the players as individuals. Each and every one of them has a different skill level and is at a different place mentally."

And so it is with discipling. You have to take the time to assess where each person is along their faith journey and respond accordingly. You need to ask yourself questions such as:

> Does this person appear to be actively growing their faith or are they just drifting along with the current?
>
> Is their faith apparent when we are together?
>
> Has s/he initiated any faith related conversations with me?
>
> Do they seem inclined to want direction from me or is it something I need to approach with a degree of caution?

Each of these questions will help you assess the most effective means of approaching them and making yourself available.

Accurate assessment of the situation will go a long way to fostering the relationship, and I assure you the best way to engage is through simple conversation. As you initiate the dialogue, and as you proceed in conversation, ask yourself this question, "Am I having a conversation or am I making a sales pitch?"

We all know what it feels like to be on the receiving end of a sales pitch, and we have all seen people trying ever so hard to convince someone to "come to the faith." My experience has been the success rate is quite low in the "sales job environment." People are much more receptive to a conversation than they are when they feel someone is trying to sell them on something.

John MacArthur really helped me when he wrote, "Are you available? Are you a worshipper? Is your intent and purpose in life focused on Christ? Having those attitudes means being controlled by the Holy Spirit who is the only One who can cause you to call Jesus Lord."[15]

I imagine it is already apparent, but I'll come right out and say it. To be effective in discipling others, you have to establish a relationship, and as the relationship develops, both of you will grow in your relationships with Christ.

True one-on-one discipling requires getting involved with your disciple. You get to know them and they get to know you. Open yourself up to them. Get vulnerable. Show your human side. Admit to weaknesses (hear me clearly—you don't need to reveal your deepest, darkest secrets, but you do have to exhibit fallibility). Give yourself to them.

First and foremost, be an example in her/his life. Remember Jesus' invitation: "Follow me"? This is the very invitation you extend when you set out to disciple someone. You invite them, "Follow me." Effectively done, they will want what you have. This is rarely stated, but often felt and observed. Oh how many times I have heard, "I don't know what it is about her, but whatever it is, I want it." I want people to say that about me... and I want to help others be that kind of person, too.

Now let's take a quick detour down Semantics Lane. One of the sacraments of my church is infant baptism, and one of the questions posed to the parents during the sacrament is, "Will you live before this child a life that becomes the gospel?"

Well before I had children, I contemplated that question, hoping one day it would be posed to me. Now, I am a bit of a word nerd, so I wondered which meaning of "becomes" was intended:

> Becomes: turns into – The caterpillar becomes a butterfly.
>
> Becomes: compliments – That dress is very becoming to you.

At the time, I decided I had a much better chance of achieving the second. I could envision myself living my life in a manner that complimented the gospel. I now realize, however, that the essential aspiration of discipleship is to live as intoned by the first definition: to live so my life evolves into the gospel (Christ-likeness). In the final analysis, the two work in tandem, but my life course has benefitted greatly by acknowledging the distinction.

One of the critical components of discipling is to live a life that becomes the gospel. Paul said it this way, *Be imitators of me, even as I also am of Christ.* (1 Corinthians 11:1). In the spirit of discipleship handed down from generation to generation, we are implored to go and do the same.

The second feature of Direct Discipling is counseling, and the most important part in this aspect of discipling is to listen. You must be dialed in to what the disciple seeks, where they want to go, and where they need to develop. One challenge here is distinguishing when you should counsel and when you should teach. Teaching relates to imparting relevant truth. Counseling also involves precisely that, but only in the context of where your friend is and where they need to go. Where are you? Where do you want to go? What is holding you back? How can I help you get there?

Before we move on, let's dwell on that second question for a moment. Where do you (the disciple) want to go? Not where I as the discipler want you to go; not where I think you should go and certainly not where I would go. The focus is on where do you want to go?

This is not to say, however, that teaching isn't a part of it. Share what you have read and learned. Share your experiences. The disciple will benefit from your knowledge, experience, and wisdom. There is definitely a call for teaching, but it must remain subordinate to counseling.

The foundation of all of this, however, is encouragement. Let me take you back to Chris, the CPA mentor I introduced you to in the last chapter. Remember I said he called me out for a spiritual gift I didn't realize I had or that it even was a spiritual gift? Well, the gift he identified in me was the gift of encouragement, or as it is phrased in some Bible translations, *exhortation.* Romans 12:6-8:

Having gifts differing according to the grace that was given to us, if prophecy, let us prophesy according to the proportion of our faith; or service, let us give ourselves to service; or he who teaches, to his teaching; or he who exhorts, to his exhorting: he who gives, let him do it with liberality; he who rules, with diligence; he who shows mercy, with cheerfulness.

Encouragement comes naturally to me, and as Chris said, it is a gift God has given me. But anyone can build their encouragement muscle. Several years ago, the trendy business management book was *The One Minute Manager* by Ken Blanchard and Spencer Johnson[16]. It's a great little volume that stands the test of time. The sticky premise that lingers with me is "Catch someone doing something right." It's so very easy to do if you just set your mind to it, and when someone does something right, call them out for it.

I had a habit when dining out that irritated my kids. I still do it, but they aren't around to be irritated anymore. When we have truly outstanding service, I always ask if I can speak to a manager when the bill comes. Invariably, the waiter shrinks away and a manager arrives filled with trepidation, inquiring what they can do for me. I then proceed to tell them what excellent service we received, and how out of the ordinary that is. I learned a long time ago, an outstanding tip gets the waiter's attention, calling their extraordinary work to the manager's attention gets them revered and maybe promoted. Why is it, I must ask, that we are so quick to call a manager over to complain about deficiencies, but rarely if ever call one over for praise?

Praise your disciple. Look for those places where they excel. I once watched a football coach ask a player during a practice drill if he knew what he just did. When the player said yes, the coach asked if he could do it again. When the player nodded, the coach said,

"Well, I want you to do that a lot!!" I am convinced the player set his mind to repeat the performance as frequently as possible.

This whole idea of Direct Discipling is well summarized by a pastor friend of mine who pleads, "Show up, suit up and build up." Show up–establish a relationship with the disciple and be intentional in doing it. Suit up–get involved, be vulnerable, listen, counsel. Build up–encourage, teach, share, help them get where they want to go.

I want to highlight the second charge there (the others are pretty self-explanatory). The first image that comes to mind is middle school gym class. "Please excuse Robert from PE today. Signed, Robert's Mom." When those notes were honored, I showed up for PE class, but didn't change into my PE clothes. I merely sat on the side and watched. Showing up wasn't enough. I needed to participate for the class to be of any benefit.

My pastor friend, though, offers a more painful example here. He shares that there were many nights when he was home for dinner with the family, but his mind was still back at the office or on the next morning's meeting. He definitely showed up for dinner, but he did not suit up. Not only was he not "on the court," he wasn't even prepared to get on the court. The conversation swirled all around him, but he wasn't in it.

I can definitely relate to that example, because I frequently did the same thing. This syndrome also applies in so many other spheres in my life—business meetings, children's athletics, or sitting in a continuing education class. I shudder when I contemplate how often I show up, but don't suit up.

Let me leave you with yet another visual. Jesus repeatedly used sheep and shepherds as examples in his teaching. One key distinction in ranching is you drive cattle and lead sheep. This is a key difference and I find not a single illustration where Jesus talks of cattle, let alone driving cattle.

No, I am not likening your mentees to cattle (and not as sheep either for that matter). The distinction here is that you will only be successful in leading them, not in driving them. A very useful question to ask them from time to time is, "What are you reading?" and its follow-up cousin, "What are you learning there?"

This pair of questions will steer your conversation to where they are and what they are wrestling with. "You must read this book (with an implied, "There will be a test when we next meet")," is not nearly as effective as offering a book relevant to the conversation they initiated with you.

When you set about Direct Discipling, you commit to showing up, suiting up and building up. It requires all three.

Indirect Discipling

Indirect Discipling takes on a different character, and it all starts with character, your character. Character is grounded in the example you set. With Indirect Discipling, there is no direct one-on-one counseling or teaching. There is only leading by example and letting your Christianity show. Whereas with Direct Discipling you lead the disciple, with Indirect Discipling you let the disciple take the initiative with you.

One example here is parenting, right? All our lives, we have heard, "Be aware of your actions, little eyes are watching." As hard as it is to believe from their behavior, even teenagers watch us, although the effects may not be visible for years.

It also carries over into the workplace where departments and organizations commonly take on the personalities of their leaders. When evaluating the internal controls in an organization (those procedures and safeguards designed to promote integrity), the first aspect an auditor evaluates is leadership. What tone is being set at the top? As goes the leadership, so goes the company. Whether you realize it or not, whether you want them to or not, others watch and follow your lead.

This is another area where I caution you not to limit your perspective. Now I expect you may well be thinking, "This doesn't apply to me, I am not in a leadership position." Many times though, the leader is not necessarily the person with authority and a title. Almost always, it is the person who has earned the respect of the others in that community. Living out your Christian faith in and of itself will earn you respect, which will raise you up as a leader.

I implore you to be intentional in setting an example worthy of following and I urge you to be constantly aware of your spiritual underpinnings. And as you grow in spiritual maturity, it should also become apparent to those around you.

This brings to mind one of my most surprising and heart-warming experiences. I had the honor of being invited back to my university to address an undergraduate class of about 200 finance students a few years ago. The requested topic for my talk was how the classroom learning during my college days paved the way for the amazing career that unfolded before me. Being in the presence of those bright students was invigorating and I was uplifted throughout the presentation.

At the end, several students came down and surrounded me, asking follow-up questions as the professor stood on the periphery of the circle listening. It was apparent from the time I walked in the room that he was "that professor." Surely you know "that professor." All colleges have at least one "that professor," the professor who truly engages with the students not only academically, but on a personal level as well.

Wholly unexpectedly, one of the students said, "I'm just inspired at how you live out your faith." I was momentarily stunned. I responded, "Really? Why do you say that? There was nothing about faith in my talk." He said, "I know, but it was apparent throughout." As I took that in, the professor looked me straight in the eye and added, "Oh, yes. It was obvious."

I can assure you, there was nothing in my presentation that even hinted of my faith, or even what religion I subscribe to. I had gone out of my way to exclude my faith from the presentation, keeping it purely secular, and it had not even entered my mind that my faith experience would have any bearing on what I had to say. Nevertheless, not-so-little eyes watched (and not so little ears heard) that day.

When we operate in this Indirect Discipling mode, we don't limit ourselves to other Christians.

At a workshop conducted by the late, great theologian Marcus Borg, he shared a great approach. Dr. Borg was, among other things, a professor at Oregon State University. During his tenure there, the school eliminated the religion college and his very popular courses were subsequently offered in the philosophy college. As a result, he drew a very diverse slice of the student body.

The story he shared was of a repetitive experience for him. It was not unusual after his first or second lecture to have a student approach him and say, "Dr. Borg, I don't believe in God."

His response, which I have embraced, was, "Tell me about this 'God' you don't believe in." The explanations generally fell into one of two categories – an uncaring, distant god or a harsh disciplinarian god. Once the student finished describing the god in whom s/he didn't believe, Dr. Borg's answer was invariably, "I don't believe in that God either."

Which highlights for me, two of the key components of Indirect Discipling: listening and being approachable. It would have been ever so easy for Dr. Borg to respond to those statements by launching into why it is essential to believe in a supreme being. It would have been natural for Dr. Borg to advocate for the Trinitarian God of the Christian faith (it certainly would have been my natural impulse), but Dr. Borg chose a different path, a more excellent path. Rather, he invited the students to share their image of God. And then he listened, and the Dr. Borg I came to know that day listened intently. He didn't listen for weaknesses in the student's explanation he could exploit. No, he listened to discern from where the student spoke, and I suspect he listened for what he might learn from each of those students.

My thoughts turn to Alister McGrath who wrote, "Arguments do not convert. They may remove obstacles to conversion and support the faith of the believer, but in and of themselves they do not possess the capacity to transform humanity. True conversion rests on an encounter with a glorious and gracious God."[17]

But these exchanges with the students started well before the question was ever posed, because Dr. Borg exuded an approachable aura. With so many professors, speakers, leaders and respected individuals, a distance exists. We know better than to cross that canyon to initiate conversation with them.

Not so with Dr. Borg. He was approachable. His demeanor invited their interaction. Here was a big-time professor—many times published and sought nationwide—yet his students felt comfortable bringing questions and inviting conversation, even early in the course. He made himself approachable!

Note also that he exerted no attempt to convert the students in his class. He exposed them to the values and ideals of the Christian faith and left the conversion to Jesus.

I am reminded that the Great Commission says, "All authority has been given to me in heaven and on earth. Go, and make disciples of all nations, baptizing them in the name of the Father and of the Son and of the Holy Spirit, teaching them to observe all things that I commanded you. Behold, I am with you always, even to the end of the age."

We often distort this exhortation as a call to pursue converts. I remind again, the charge here is to share the gospel, to be cultivators, not convertors. We are to share the word and leave the conversion to Christ. In this way, we provide a pathway between the person and God.

Before we move on, I want to stress one more point of emphasis. Indirect Discipling is not a passive endeavor. Identifying people we might influence merely going about our business and being mindful of them is not the drill here. You need to actively assess where they are and how you can help them grow spiritually. The distinction from Direct Discipling is that you don't directly engage in the process with them.

I have a friend who taught elementary school for many years. We discussed the current state of public education that barred from the school environment any introduction of religious teaching. She said, "Just because I can't use religion in my teaching doesn't mean I'm not teaching my Christian principles. I can no longer tell them 'Do unto others as they do unto you,' but I can still tell them to treat others as they want to be treated. I can't tell them 'Thou shalt not steal and Thou shalt not covet,' but you can be assured that I constantly tell them not to take what isn't theirs and to be satisfied with what they have, not to yearn for what their classmate has."

She was Indirectly Disicpling her students. She actively assessed where they were and what would develop their spiritual growth. She was not only intentional in her efforts, but she also took action. In no way was it passive.

A second passing example I would give you is Chris whom I described in The Indirect Discipling section of Chapter 4. Chris was Indirectly Discipling the room of CPAs by leading with his Christian foundation. There was nothing devious or deceptive in his methods; he was merely sharing what he believed in a non-confrontational manner.

Now hop back with me to the list you developed at the beginning of this chapter. The real work with the list comes in your Indirect Discipling. Periodically revisit this list. With care and attention, you will become increasingly aware of people you are Indirectly Discipling, and more importantly people you could/should be Indirectly Discipling. Even so, your Overlookeds list should expand as you become more aware and more proficient in your Indirect Discipling, leading you to others that lie just outside your reach. You will also occasionally find people moving from Overlooked to Followers and from Followers to Disciples. Be assured, however, if no one crosses over, it is in no way an indication of a failed, or failing discipling ministry.

I noted before that the folks you elect to disciple in Indirect Discipling should take the initiative in the relationship. This is not to say there are no exceptions to the rule. As your awareness and sensitivity increase, you too will notice opportunities that are ripe for initiating a conversation. Luther Ivory observed, "Without having to earn it, we were called each day and invited to sit at a table prepared by someone we knew and loved us unconditionally."[18] We are to prepare the same table and present it to others, and in the process to love them unconditionally. This is at the heart of discipleship.

So now we have covered both of the discipleship dimensions: being discipled and discipling others. It's time to commit.

Disciple is indeed a verb.

Study Questions

Which was more difficult for you, identifying the people who are discipling you or in identifying whom you are discipling? Why?

As you examined your relationships, were there any you previously didn't see as discipling relationships and now do?

Acknowledging the influence you have over others is powerful. Name some ways you can use this influence for the good of someone in your life.

All of us have good days and bad days, but is your general default state one of joy? After you've been with someone, even for just a minute or two, do they walk away with the impression you were joyful or just business? (If you want to test your answer, ask your spouse.)

Acknowledging the concept of the Overlookeds can be life-changing. Are you willing to take on the challenge? If so, what can you do to heighten your awareness of whom you are overlooking?

What are the escape hatches you most often use to rationalize not engaging someone in discipleship?

What are the indicators that distinguish a

conversation from a sales pitch? How do you know when a chat has shifted from conversation to sales pitch? From a sales pitch to a conversation?

CHAPTER 6
The Committed Disciple

In this is my Father glorified, that you bear much fruit; and so you will be my disciples. Even as the Father has loved me, I also have loved you. Remain in my love. If you keep my commandments, you will remain in my love; even as I have kept my Father's commandments, and remain in his love. I have spoken these things to you, that my joy may remain in you, and that your joy may be made full. This is my commandment, that you love one another, even as I have loved you.

John 15:8-12

It was character that got us out of bed, commitment that moved us into action, and discipline that enabled us to follow through.

Zig Ziglar

I've said it before, but I can't say it too often. Be intentional!

And now it's time to talk about intentionality's partner: commitment.

Entering into these discipling relationships must be grounded in commitment and this commitment comes in three parts: commitment to yourself, commitment to God, and commitment to your discipleship relationships. You can follow Christ casually, but if you truly seek to fulfill your discipleship calling, you must commit to yourself, God, and the Discipleship Road journey.

Commitment to Yourself

When I reflect on my commitment to becoming a disciple of Jesus, the first thought that comes to mind is the commitment to God and his purposes, but the first commitment must be to yourself. Only when you have fortified that commitment, can you turn your attention to committing to God.

Remember, God's command to Moses, *You shall love your neighbor as yourself.* (Leviticus 19:18), which Jesus carried forward when he reminded the people, *You shall love your neighbor as yourself.* (Mark 5:19 and Matthew 19:19)

Note the foundation of this command in self-love. You cannot fully love others until you embrace the love from within. This is the converse of Jesus' parable where he tells the people, *Why do you see the speck of chaff that is in your brother's eye, but don't consider the beam that is in your own eye?* (Luke 6:41)

In that parable, he called them out for being critical of the flaws and shortcomings of others, when their flaws and shortcomings far exceeded those of the others. In his command to Moses, he affirms the other side. We cannot truly see the beauty in others until we first embrace our own beauty. And God created each of us beautiful.

Our God the Creator, is the creator of all things beautiful and wondrous. We cannot be reminded often enough that we are created in his image, and God's image is one of love and beauty, and to be created in God's image is to bear an image of love and beauty. Your calling therefore is to love and create. And it is in embracing your beauty that you are released to love and to create.

While we are indeed created in God's image, we remain imperfect creations and we embark on the journey on Discipleship Road in order to move towards Godly perfection. In the chapters that follow, we will explore specific ways to grow closer to Christ and reclaim our Godly nature, but that journey begins in your commitment to growing in God's image in order to become the person God designed you to be.

It's easy to yield to temptation and delay this journey until we have our houses in order, but that is nothing more than a stalling technique. You are to start right where you are right now. Build on your beliefs and your relationship with God just as it is. He is eager to meet you where you stand and he will empower you to help others even as he guides you.

Directly stated, get started today in the two phases of discipleship we have previously addressed: being discipled and discipling others.

With your face turned to God and hand-in-hand with other pilgrims on Discipleship Road, you are ready to connect with God's power.

Commitment to God

Embracing your created image and acknowledging your place in God's family prepares you to present yourself to God. In his second letter to Timothy, Paul implored Timothy to, *Give diligence to present yourself approved by God, a workman who doesn't need to be ashamed, properly handling the Word of Truth.* (2 Timothy 2:15)

Let's break it down:

Give diligence – Diligence: Endeavors intentionally pursued with dedication driving towards a predetermined result. Not undertaken lightly.

To present yourself – These endeavors are not as much about a call to obedience, but rather living your life in a manner that enables you to take the initiative and present yourself to your Creator.

Approved by God, as a workman – Here again, we find further affirmation this is something you work at, not a dalliance of convenience. You engage in the work as a workman, not as a casual participant. Also, the term workman invokes the notion of a craft to be honed and perfected.

Who does not need to be ashamed – You are called to be a witness for Christ, and not ashamed. Your workmanship will sculpt you into a confident ambassador for Jesus. When you are diligent and commit to Christian workmanship, you will stand before God without shame.

Accurately handling the Word of Truth – Accurate: Correct and precise. No one, not even the accomplished theologian N. T. Wright, will profess a complete command of the scriptures. While God's Word is timeless and unchanging, it is simultaneously evergreen and open to rediscovery by each new generation in the context of the time and culture of our ever-changing world. Accurate handling calls for constant wrestling with the Word on your own and in concert with other disciples.

In his book *On the Anvil*, Max Lucado likens us to tools in the hands of the Master, and he identifies three states of existence. "We are all somewhere in the blacksmith's shop. We are either on the scrap pile, in the Master's hands on the anvil, or in the tool chest." [19]

In other words, we are either of no use and just gathering dust, getting transformed into a useful state, or ready for service. The unashamed, approved workman who accurately handles the Word of Truth is a tool the Master can use to craft his kingdom here on earth as it is in heaven.

Commit to God and be transformed.

Commit to Being Discipled

When it comes to discipleship, the choices are all yours. You can choose to be a follower; you can choose to be a disciple; you can choose to decline the invitation... you can even decide not to decide. Most assuredly the choice God calls you to, however, is discipleship.

Committing to being discipled is a commitment to learning and changing. A quick review of Chapter 4 will reveal the underlying foundation for this commitment.

Maximizing your opportunities for growth comes through the counsel of others only when you commit to their guidance, not by way of an on-again, off-again proposition. Paul repeatedly uses physical training metaphors drawing the connection that much as we must physically train to build our bodies, so must we train spiritually to nurture our souls. Very little is achieved through the cycle of joining a gym at the first of the year, becoming disinterested and dropping out in February, and taking it up again in May. Similarly, you must constantly strive to become the person God sees in you, therefore a casual attitude will not achieve the results you expect. Intentionality and commitment.

Equally significant, you must remain respectful of the investment your Spiritual Guides make in you. I guarantee you they invest in you out of joy and love for Christ, but be attentive to ensure they have no opportunities to feel their efforts are wasted.

You must also find an appropriate balance in these relationships. When you connect with these individuals, the temptation is to go all in, seeking their guidance at every turn. You can easily become a pest. So I challenge you to remain respectful of their needs and constraints, allowing the relationship to develop naturally as you discover an appropriate balance.

I wish I could provide you the magic formula to attain this balance, but I have yet to distill it, and I seriously doubt it can be reduced to an equation or algorithm. The appropriate frequency of your exchanges will vary from relationship to relationship.

One of my Spiritual Guides is someone I see weekly and often call or email between visits. In contrast, one of my longest and most reliable Spiritual Guides moved to another city years ago. I only see him once or twice a year and we talk or email sporadically, sometimes going two or three months between contacts. Nevertheless, he influences me daily through the lessons I have learned from our relationship.

My advice to you is:

> Start slowly,
> Be respectful of their schedules,
> When in doubt, ask, and
> Watch for non-verbal clues which indicate an interest in their increasing or decreasing their investment in your relationship.

I also need to make a few observations about clergy as Spiritual Guides. Some of your best guidance will come from ordained ministers, and your interactions with them will vary depending on those relationships. I have long-standing relationships that developed over the years with many pastors and a couple of new relationships that are just forming. At least three pastors are Directly Discipling me right now (each in a different aspect of my spiritual growth) and an estimated three others are Indirectly Discipling me.

Be respectful of the many demands on their time. As you get to know pastors, you gain insight into just how stressful their jobs are. Obviously, they devote significant time to study and prepare sermons. All clergy are also involved in managing staff whether organizing and leading laity as an Associate Pastor, or in managing the full-time, part-time and volunteer staff as a Senior Pastor. Add in the demands of running the business end of the church and you arrive at the profile for a very demanding job.

Additionally, much, if not all, of the congregation looks to them for spiritual direction, not to mention personal attention in times of crisis (which come at all hours of the day and night). And most often overlooked is their commitment to their families. Truly, a pastor's work is never done.

My recommendations for building successful disciplee/discipler relationships with clergy include:

Never forget it is a relationship and remember all successful relationships are two-way streets. You seek guidance and knowledge and in return you need to be supportive and encouraging of the pastor. Be there for her/him.

Remain mindful of the demands on their time, requesting time respectfully with the expectation that you will likely be asked to wait until availability opens on her/his schedule. Do not take this as an indication that your spiritual growth is unimportant to them, but rather that there are many other people pulling on their time.

View the exchanges as a highly privileged gift. I regard each of my pastor relationships to be in the style of the rabbis of Jesus' time. The opportunity to sit at their feet and learn was a privilege then, one to be revered, and so it is for me as well as for the pastors who disciple me.

Commitment to Discipling Others

Not surprisingly, many of the considerations in assessing your commitment to discipling another person are the same ones discussed in the section immediately above (e.g., respect for each other's time, availability, open and honest communication). The disciple, rather than you, should drive the relationship, although you definitely have a say regarding pace. You need to find the delicate balance between being attentive and not burning yourself out. A quick review of Chapter 5 will provide insights as to what is expected of you as a discipler.

As the discipler, remain prepared for occasional overzealousness from your disciple. This often occurs at the outset, but can also kick in along the way. Typically, when I (as a disciple) connect with a new Spiritual Guide, my enthusiasm spikes. I get all excited about new territory I have discovered through the relationship and my thoughts swirl around whatever it is we are working through. This can manifest itself in my wearing out my welcome with them.

When you sense the relationship with your disciple is headed in this direction, address it early on. Don't let resentment invade your relationship. Recognize this intensity for what it is: the disciplee's profound appreciation for your investment in them and their excitement in growing in Christ. Don't douse their enthusiasm, but address the need to create space for both of you to breathe.

The disciplee's passion can also spike later in the

relationship, virtually at any time. There are many root causes, but the two most common are *a)* when they experience a breakthrough in their faith, and *b)* a significant event in their lives. I well remember a time years ago, when I had tilled new soil daily in my faith journey, and almost weekly I had some breakthrough revelation about a scriptural detail. I would rush to a particular Spiritual Guide of mine, gushing out what I had uncovered.

More often than not, his response was, "Interesting yes, but does it significantly alter your understanding of who Jesus is?"

Most of the time, it did not.

With regard to significant life events, these are almost always unexpected (the primary exception that comes to mind is becoming a parent, for which you typically get nine-months of advance warning). A death in the family, marriage, job change, and/or moving your residence all trigger new thoughts and relationships. The most common effect is the disciplee requires a little more breathing room to adjust to the change. Honor that need, but stay connected and available, realizing these times also provide opportunities for great spiritual growth. Conversely, these events can drive the disciplee to find themselves seeking more guidance and direction. Make every effort to help them in these times of transition.

Another critical acknowledgement comes in allowing them to set the pace. Your primary job is to be accessible. Sure, you will check in with them occasionally, but only in the interest of gauging their temperature and to remind them you are available. You don't want to be too persistent here, lest you come off as over-aggressive.

Much like being discipled, I have found that frequency of contact varies with each relationship. In of one of my closest discipling relationships where I am the discipler, we meet every 6-8 weeks, and talk/email once or twice between visits, depending on what is going on in our lives. On the other hand, I have another disciplee whom I see no less than once a week (many weeks it's more like two or three times) and we email daily. Different strokes for different folks. In summary, no one size fits all exists in these relationships.

Engaging in discipleship, both as the disciplee and as the discipler, calls for commitment. Keep this in mind as we move on to explore disciplines that will build your commitment to yourself.

Disciple is a verb!

STUDY QUESTIONS

Discuss the distinction between a casual relationship and a committed relationship.

Confront the temptation to wait until "you have your house in order" before committing to God.

Robert cites Max Lucado's three states of tools in the blacksmith's shop.
In which state are you currently?

Can you think of times when you were in the other states?

What obstacles prevent you from a deeper commitment to discipleship? What do you need to overcome? What do you need to let go of?

Is there intentionality in your commitment to the people you disciple – both directly and indirectly?

CHAPTER 7
Discipleship Disciplines

For I desire to have you know how greatly I struggle for you, and for those at Laodicea, and for as many as have not seen my face in the flesh; that their hearts may be comforted, they being knit together in love, and gaining all riches of the full assurance of understanding, that they may know the mystery of God, both of the Father and of Christ, in whom are all the treasures of wisdom and knowledge hidden.

Now this I say that no one may delude you with persuasiveness of speech. For though I am absent in the flesh, yet am I with you in the spirit, rejoicing and seeing your order, and the steadfastness of your faith in Christ. As therefore you received Christ Jesus, the Lord, walk in him, rooted and built up in him, and established in the faith, even as you were taught, abounding in it in thanksgiving. Be careful that you don't let anyone rob you through his philosophy and vain deceit, after the tradition of men, after the elements of the world, and not after Christ.

Colossians 2:1-8

Holy habits are that: the disciplines, the routines by which we stay alive and focused on Him. At first we choose them and carry them out; after a while they are part of who we are. And they carry us.
Mark Buchanan

Building relationships is the key to growing as a disciple of Christ, but it is not the sole focus. Much of being discipled is about what the other person does for you. In this chapter, we will explore, ever so briefly, critical aspects over which you have to take ownership–namely prayer, Bible study, meditation and reflection, fasting and worship.

Prayer – The primary, fundamental building block to growing in your faith is prayer, and prayer comes in many forms each appropriate to a given circumstance. There are long meditative prayers, short prayers for strength, prayers before meals, prayers for others, prayers for wisdom—the list goes on.

One thing is certain. No one methodology fits all circumstances. There is so much to be said about prayer, more than we can do justice to here, but let's visit a few highlights.

What is prayer, after all? The best definition I have found is "conversation in the presence of God." More than anything else, God wants to have an intimate relationship with you and, much like any other intimate relationship, it lives or dies on communication. Any time you find yourself speaking in the presence of God, you are in prayer.

Prayer in this context is like a physical muscle. The more you exercise it and the more you develop its abilities, the stronger it becomes and the more you can rely on it. Much like a physical workout routine, the more you work at prayer, the more natural it becomes.

Just a few years ago, a lady I knew well, a true Spiritual Guide for many of us, had a completely unexpected heart attack in the normal course of her day and died in her mid-fifties. It shocked us all.

At her funeral, one of the people who brought a testimony shared that she started every morning in prayer. She got her Bible, her journal, and a full cup of coffee before she settled in for two hours working her prayer lists every morning. I remember thinking, "That must be amazing. What does one find to pray about for two hours? Not to mention carving out time to do so." I just couldn't shake thinking about what that would entail.

It pushed me to a new commitment to a morning prayer time that now begins my day focused on God and centered on our relationship. I start every day tuning into WGOD. I dial into his broadcast. I'll also admit that it isn't too long into the day that someone changes the channel (and that person is usually me).

I initially committed to devoting 10 minutes (10 precious minutes) each morning to prayer, and I maintained a prayer list, first mentally and later in writing. In the beginning, I found it difficult to stay on task for 10 minutes. My mind kept jumping to other subjects, most often to the events that lay ahead in my day. My mind would take off in unexpected directions. I learned that if I would just steer it back to God, the prayer could continue. I also came to realize that many of those "distractions" were the result of God taking our conversation where he wanted it, in contrast to where I thought it should go.

Over time I found that I couldn't get the job done in 10 minutes so 10 minutes stretched into 20, and 20 into 30 and 30 into 45. I am now up to about an hour a morning and it is the most relaxing, liberating hour of my day, and I never run out of things to talk with God about.

Will I ever get to the two-hour discipline she had? I don't know, but I assure you, when I started out, an hour seemed so far out of reach I couldn't even aspire to it. I also can't tell you where the extra time came from to engage in this discipline. I just know it did.

My morning prayer time is not sufficient for the day. Not an hour goes by that some incident doesn't occur that draws me back into prayer. It could be some great achievement, or some difficulty a friend has encountered, or an accident on the freeway. Sometimes, I get an email or text from someone asking for prayer in the moment to get them through some immediate challenge. Rare is the situation where I can't take 30 or 60 seconds right then to pray into their request. And most nights end with a closing prayer for the day as I drift off to sleep.

You may already be at the two-hour-a-day commitment in your prayer discipline. You may be where I was at that funeral thinking 10 minutes a day was your limit and expanding the process wasn't for you. I challenge you to give it a try for 30 days and see if your life isn't changed.

And don't forget, prayer is a conversation, a two-way dialogue. I love this exchange from Bruce Main's *If Jesus Were a Senior, Last Minute Preparations for a Post-Collegiate Life*:

"I'm tired of your complaining," came the Voice beside me. I had not seen anyone when I first entered the empty chapel. I wanted to get away. I wanted to escape. The last thing I wanted was to talk. "I know what you are thinking," continued the Intruder. "You've come here to pray and get away from it all. Well, guess what, you're not the only one who gets to talk. If you're going to pray, you better get ready to listen, too." I do not like the attitude of my intrusive Friend – always showing up at inappropriate moments and places. A chapel, of all places![20]

Can you relate? I surely can!

Meditation and reflection - Meditation and reflection are close cousins to prayer. In general, they both involve retreating from your daily activities to a place where you can focus your thoughts on God and matters of the soul.

Meditation can take many forms. Whereas prayer is usually heavy on the talking and lighter on the listening, meditation is predominantly about the listening augmented by an occasional response. Meditation for me comes when I quiet my mind and soul so I can focus on God. For me, it is not a formal process, although I acknowledge those methods have been effective for others.

To get started, I select a point of focus to start my meditation. It can be a scripture passage, a lyric from a song, or some theological concept that confounds me. I fix my mind on that topic and listen for God. Rare indeed are the occasions where he doesn't take over from there. It is as if he is constantly waiting on tiptoe to be invited in.

Reflection is very, very similar. Here again, I need to withdraw from the world's distractions so I can turn to a specific theme (at least at the outset) where the listening predominates. Reflection, however, tends to be more introspective. It usually centers on some event that has occurred, most often some behavior of mine. The natural tendency is to focus on some situation I didn't handle well, but it can just as easily be some euphoric event that I want to revisit to discern its deeper relevance. I start with a recent experience which then rolls into what it portends for the future and how I can make the best of whatever happened. With a little reflection, I can often turn a negative into a positive or a positive into something glorious.

I have yet to develop these disciplines into a routine. Prayer is habitual—every day. Meditation and reflection are opportunistic for me. I seize the chance to engage in them when it arises. Well, more accurately I jump into these activities when the opportunity arises and I realize it is upon me. Far too often, the opportunity arose well after the moment has passed. Clearly, this is a muscle I need to develop.

Bible Study – It should come as no surprise to

you that Bible study is part and parcel of growing your faith. Effective prayer, meditation, and reflection are all anchored in Biblical principles and you can't pray, meditate, or reflect on Biblical principles unless you seek a better understanding of what the Bible is telling you.

You must also acknowledge the Bible is a multifaceted work. It is simultaneously a book of rules, a grand history book, a literary wonder, and a collection of love letters from God. From time to time, we need to step back and read it through each of these four lenses. The lens through which we read impacts how we respond, and reading from each of these lenses will draw you closer to God as you come to understand the many ways in which he approaches you. The words don't change, but how you hear them shifts as you change your perspective lens.

Most simply though, you need to read the Bible. You need to read the Bible and marinate in its messages and embrace its promises. Whether you seek answers, look for guidance or just try to fathom the God we worship, you need to read the Bible.

Granted, the Bible contains many rules, commandments, and guidelines for living, but above all it is a book of promises, and you can't live a life grounded in the confidence of God's promises unless you read the Bible to know what they are. And once you begin to grasp the peace and joy that comes through those promises, you will feel a natural urge to share that peace and joy with others.

Like the other disciplines we are exploring in this section, Bible study is a muscle that strengthens the more you engage it. Similar to the prayer habit, I started out with 10 minutes of Bible reading each morning—actually, the prayer habit was an extension of my Bible reading. I started out committing 10 minutes a morning to Bible reading. It wasn't long before I wanted to stay in the Bible a little longer so I upped the commitment to 20 minutes. Well, then I wanted to add in other Christian writings, so I expanded to 30 minutes, ensuring that no less than 10 of those minutes were in the Bible itself. It was way too tempting to just spend the full 30 minutes in other Christian writing on some days, but I realized I needed the Bible every day. About that time I added the prayer time to the morning reading and both grew together from there.

The more I read the Bible and explore the writings of those who have devoted their lives to studying the Bible, the more I realize how much I have yet to learn. Every revelation seems to open doors to a dozen new perplexities. I then wrestle with those. The more I wrestle, the more I enjoy engaging in the exercise.

The more I read, the more I want to know, and it builds from there. As Wes Westrum, a one-time manager of the New York Mets, observed, "Baseball is like church—many attend, but few understand."

I added my own corollary, "The more I understand, the more I understand just how little I understand." This became a wonderful cycle for me—reading and learning → my comprehension falling short → hunger for more learning → reading and learning → repeat. It has truly been a never-ending quest . . . and I LOVE it!

"How can that be?" you wonder. "Where does the time come from? I could never find a spare hour every day. I have a demanding job and family duties, not to mention church commitments."

These were my very thoughts at the time, but I assure you, you have the time. When I started this morning routine, I was Vice President Finance and Chief Financial Officer for a major professional sports franchise. Sixty-hour workweeks were the norm, and the demands of many weeks well exceeded the norm. I had two children in school for which I shared parenting duties while coaching their baseball and soccer teams, and we found time for church. Our kids definitely had a drug problem—I drug them to church every Sunday. (Yes it's an old joke, but hey, the shoe fits.)

I suspect many if not most of you find time to go to the gym most days, and I'm willing to bet when you first started, you absolutely knew there were not enough hours in the day to get in a workout, but you committed to start small just to see where it led. The same is true with growing spiritually. Paul entreated us not only to build the body, but also to build the soul.

You also have the autonomy to tailor your study and prayer time to fit your schedule. I settled into a pattern of 3½ hours a week minimum for the reading component, with no less than 10 minutes each day. This way, I can go short on mornings when I have an early meeting and then make up the time later in the week. Here again, I had to build in a discipline enforcing mechanism. I found myself falling behind at times and "banking" hours at others. Before long, I found there was no discipline to my discipline. In reality, I was just keeping score, so I decided each week would stand on its own—no rollover minutes. I did, however, retain the minimum daily requirement of 10 minutes and the 3½ hour minimum weekly commitment.

I also stated this is a morning exercise, because that is simply what works best for me. It may not work well for you. Maybe you can isolate yourself midday at lunch. Maybe evenings are better for you. Find the time that works best for you, preferably at the time of day when you do your best work. After all, you want to give yourself to God when you are at your best, not when you are distracted or unable to focus on your relationship with him.

I settled on mornings for several reasons. If I set the alarm a little earlier, I could have the living room or study to myself before the kids started stirring and the day whirring. When I read the paper or my email first, my mind took off on the day's events and ran away without me, so I established a routine of rolling out of bed and heading straight to my place of study, which originally was in the living room, but has since moved to my study.

Midday didn't work for me because, although I was a senior executive, I never seemed to gain full control over my calendar. Try as I might to schedule efficiently, more often than not I found myself a slave to the day's schedule rather than master of it. Evenings? Not a chance. Come home from work, catch up on the family's events of the day, dinner, homework (theirs and mine), chores, etc. Not to mention the inclination to succumb and let myself get distracted and unfocussed in the evenings.

Some find late at night to be optimal. It doesn't work for me. By the time I got to the end of the day, I hadn't the energy or focus to do the devotions justice. Most prayers started well and ended with snoring.

For me, mornings are ideal. Now my kids are grown and on their own, and early morning is still the time I look forward to. Me and my God. I talk to him and I know he listens. He talks to me and he hopes I listen. It is so easy for me to fall into a pattern of doing all the talking, but true prayer is dialogue with both parties speaking and if it is going to bear fruit, both parties need to be listening… and I have no doubt which one of us is lacking on listening.

I'm going to paraphrase Paul here and urge you to listen without ceasing.

And I'll share one more tidbit. Long ago, and many times since, I heard stewardship pleas that assured me if I gave to the church, I would never be in need financially. Many, many testimonies about how someone didn't believe they could budget for stretch giving and not collapse their household budget only to find that all their budgetary needs (needs, not wants) got met. Well, I have had the same experience with regard to time. When I get too busy for my morning time with God, I find the hurrieder I go, the behinder I get. When I ensure my quiet times are honored, time seems to expand to accommodate the tasks of the day. I can't explain it. All I can tell you is I have experienced it, and experienced it consistently.

When things take an unexpected turn, which

seems to occur just about every day, I have fallen into the practice of asking myself, "Where is God in this? What is the lesson here?"

Granted, I'm not consistent with it yet, but I'm becoming more spiritually aware. I assure you much more is learned when I do so than when I "curse the darkness." My tendency is to apply this technique when things turn against me, but it works equally well when something unexpectedly positive occurs. I am learning God is always in there somewhere if only I will slow down long enough to look for him and truly seek his message.

Fasting – I am baffled by the mystery of fasting, or rather the lack thereof. Fasting is a mainstay in both the Old and New Testaments. People of faith are repeatedly called to fasting in times of challenge and difficulty. The gospels not only cite Jesus teaching on fasting, but also engaging in it. The mystery for me is if it were important enough for Jesus to practice it and teach it, and it was significant enough for the gospel writers to include it in their books, and if we are serious about the business of living Christ-like lives, why is there no focus on the practice today?

Jesus prayed and taught us how to pray and we ardently follow those examples. Jesus fasted and taught on fasting, yet we give it hardly a passing thought.

I have reflected on this conundrum and concluded the disconnect largely results from our inability to internalize the benefits of fasting. Personally, I find at least two great benefits from engaging in fasting. The first is the discipline of fasting develops an ability to gain control over my body. As you become more effective in fasting, your urges to respond to food stimuli come under your control. Until you set your mind to watch for food enticements, you won't realize how constant they are. We are bombarded with pleas to "eat here," "buy this sandwich," "follow our diet plan." Fast for a day and spend the evening watching broadcast TV (ABC, CBS, NBC). You will be amazed at the temptations they parade by you in a single evening.

The other benefit is that when you engage in fasting, the hunger urges come, many at first, but fewer as you grow the fasting muscle. Even as an experienced faster, you will grow hungry, and you can use each such moment as a reminder of your relationship with God and turn your thoughts to him.

Worship – Worship is game day! We were created to worship, and worship is a team sport. (I mean corporate worship here, of course.) As we would for any team sport, we train on our own (prayer, meditation and reflection, Bible study, and fasting) in preparation for worship. Like all team sports each of us has strengths that equip us to play our position in the worship experience (some teach, some sing, some preach, some pray, some encourage). While we can certainly worship by ourselves, it all comes together when we all come together.

Nothing like a spirited worship service ratchets up your discipleship. We often stumble in thinking the worship service is for us, hoping the music is sufficiently uplifting while we wait for an inspired sermon. This is not the purpose of the worship service. The purpose of the worship experience is... WORSHIP! We are there to worship God.

Said in another context, we are there to practice worshiping God. The Bible is most emphatic that our job in the next life is to worship the Almighty. "Holy, holy, holy is the Lord God, the Almighty, who was and who is and who is to come!" In corporate worship, we get to practice worshiping God and in so doing we experience his presence.

* * * * *

There you have the five basic Discipleship Disciplines. There are others, and as you proceed down Discipleship Road, you will discover others you wish to employ.

One I aspire to develop is to clear time midday each day to reset and focus on God. I'm not seeking to carve out an extended meditation period; I'm just looking to insert a pause for prayer and focus. The concept is to take a very few minutes to reflect on the morning devotion time and the events that have transpired throughout the morning. This sounds like it would be easy to implement, but for the life of me I continually fail. I start the morning and commit to stop sometime around noon. The next thought I have in that regard is when I am on the drive home, "Rats! I missed it again!"

I am convinced this midday reset will pay great dividends, as I am reminded of my Baptist brethren who hold Wednesday night prayer meetings. I have no doubts that Wednesday was not a day selected out of convenience; it was intentionally set right in the middle in the week to provide the spiritual booster shot to bridge Sunday to Sunday. Personally, I try to meet with two men's groups each week, one on Thursday mornings, and the other on Friday mornings. It always amazes me how drained my spiritual batteries get by Sunday when I miss these meetings.

Mark Hall of Casting Crowns nailed it for me in the midst of their concert on the Casting Crowns "The Altar and the Door Tour." Mark shared that when he is at the altar during worship, he is ever close to his savior. They are one, but by the time the worship experience is over and he reaches the back door of the church, he already feels a distance between him and Christ. Amen, brother! That is the exact syndrome I seek to fight with these interposed daily moments to refocus on Christ. I so wish I had succeeded in getting these midday moments in my daily routine, but I just haven't gotten there yet. Clearly I have more work to do.

So now you have sharpened your focus on these five discipleship disciplines – prayer, meditation and reflection, Bible study, fasting, and worship. You're gaining confidence and feeling stronger in your faith experience. "So what?" you might ask. The purpose of growing your faith is to be an ambassador for Christ in the world, to breathe in his grace in service of pouring it out on others.

Now, before we move on, let me emphasize that these are all means to an end; they are not a template for a score sheet to assess your faithfulness. This is the error of the Pharisees. Jesus was not at all disappointed in their commitment to the commandments and laws. His frustration was they got so caught up in following the laws that they left love and compassion behind. The whole purpose of the commandments and laws was to invoke love and compassion. Do not get so caught up in these Discipleship Disciplines that you leave Jesus and love for others behind.

So how will you know you if are growing in faith?

Discipleship Fruit

The most effective means to determine if your faith is growing is characterized by Paul's fruit of the spirit in Galatians 5:22-23. The fruit of the spirit is evidenced by love, joy, peace, kindness, goodness, faithfulness, gentleness, and self-control.

Let's look at each of these ever so briefly, firmly rooted in the understanding that the Holy Spirit dwells within you and will bring forth these characteristics.

Love – God loved us even before we acknowledged his existence. Jesus died for us even when we were still sinners. God pours his love into us constantly and we are to channel it out to those we encounter—friends, family, strangers, believers, and even those who don't believe. We are to share God's love with everyone, even the unlovable.

Joy – There is a big difference in joy and happiness. The U. S. Constitution exalts the pursuit of happiness and it is indeed worthy of pursuing. The greater calling, however, is to seek joy. Joy overwhelms us at times. We are to cherish times of joy, and we need to seek opportunities to bring joy into the lives of others. This should be our constant focal point.

Peace – We all possess an inner drive for peace, even though our lifestyles argue to the contrary. Our culture pushes us to constant unrest, the drive to have more, to be more and to aspire to more. God calls us to peace. Jesus said, "My peace I leave to you." That was his parting gift to us, along with the Holy Spirit, of course. But while he graced us with this great gift, his intention was for us to carry it to others and to introduce it into their lives – "Blessed are the peacemakers."

Patience – Here is one most of us struggle with, me for sure. While the experts tell us patience is a virtue, in the day-to-day it is anything but. "Hurry up!" is one of the very first commands our children learn. "Hurry up! We're going to be late." "Hurry up, we have to get to school." "Hurry up! Everyone is waiting on us." Jesus, however, set the mark here. Jesus was never in a hurry. He knew there was plenty of time in the day and ample time in his life (even though it would be cut short) to accomplish everything he needed to do. I have also noticed when I am patient, those around me are less stressed. When I amp up, they tense up. Patience is contagious.

Kindness – Early in adulthood, I felt kindness was overrated. Who cares if I am kind, we need to get stuff done in order to achieve our objectives! (A close relative to Hurry up!) A pastor once told us that delivering the truth without love is the most damaging thing we can do; however, when we deliver the truth with a healthy dose of love, it is life affirming. I have also come to the realization that achievement absent compassion can be equally destructive. Kindness tends to follow the pattern of patience, in that the more kindness we exhibit, the more kindness we are likely to observe around us.

Goodness – Martin Luther King, Jr. said, "The time is always right to do the right thing." He hits right to the heart of goodness. Doing the right thing. The prophet Micah told us what God wants from us, *to act justly* [goodness], *to love mercy* [kindness] *and to walk humbly with your God* [faithfulness]. Goodness is what we should be all about. When goodness blossoms, it evolves into holiness.

Faithfulness – Our society thrives on success. Everything is evaluated by some success measurement. God, on the other hand, calls us to faithfulness. I remind you, God does not call us to be successful; he calls us to be faithful. Faithfulness is what this book is all about. How you can be more faithful? How can others and I help you grow in your faithfulness? How can you nurture others to grow in their faithfulness?

Gentleness – Here's another one for which I had no use early in life. What good comes from being gentle? It's the hard-driving, successful executive who gets things done. The driven athlete is the one who demolishes the competition. As I grow in maturity and in wisdom, I now realize there are indeed times that call for the hard-nosed mindset, but there are far more times where a gentle spirit can accomplish so much more.

Try this short exercise:

1) Think of times in the Bible when Jesus dealt harshly with someone. Was it effective?

2) Now think of times where Jesus extended gentleness. Was it effective?

3) Did you come up with more instances where he employed harshness or where he was gentle?

4) Which cases left the more lasting impression on you?

I implore you to become more Christ-like in your life—strive for gentleness in all your dealings.

Self-control – This one always seemed out of place to me, but as I became attentive to it, I came to appreciate its incredible power. My wife can maintain her cool, no matter what the situation. Metaphorically she can walk through the fireworks factory on fire, find the trapped workers, lead them to safety, and say, "Somebody should do something about all this smoke!" It is an amazing trait. When we panic and spread messages of doom and destruction, others follow us deep into distress. When we remain calm and trust in God's benevolence, we are so much better equipped to clear-headedly develop an optimal solution and find the ability to lead others through the difficulty.

Love, joy, peace, patience, kindness, goodness, faithfulness, gentleness, and self-control—Paul's fruit of the spirit. These are the metrics by which we can gauge our growth in faith.

Now you have a work plan for constant improvement. Let's talk about duration.

I reiterate – Disciple is a verb.

STUDY QUESTIONS

Is prayer as conversation with God how you think of prayer? Are your prayers dialogues or monologues?

Do you invest time in meditation and reflection? Is this what is intended by "Be still and know that I am God"?

Do you perceive the Bible as a book of rules or a book of promises?

Do you employ Bible study in your regimen?
If not, whom can you turn to that might get you started in an effective and infectious way?
If so, do you agree with Robert's corollary to the Wes Westrum statement (The more I understand, the more I understand just how little I understand.)?

Is your relationship with God and spiritual development worthy of a 20-minute investment each day? What 20-minute commitments do you currently have in your daily routine? Is each of them more important than your relationship with God and spiritual development? What time of day do you find optimal for committing to these spiritual disciplines? Why does that time work best for you?

Do you engage in fasting at all? Why do you

believe it is so seldom employed today? Will you consider experimenting with fasting? If so, what purpose will it serve for you?

Reflect on your typical worship experience. Are you there to get filled up and recharged or are you there to celebrate God and to sing his praises?

Which of the dimensions of the fruit of the spirit are your weak points? What intentional steps can you take to improve? What others come to mind?

Are there specific situations where you excel with the eight fruits of the spirit character traits? In what situations are you are most susceptible to weakness?

Robert McBurnett

CHAPTER 8
A Disciple for Life

But we are bound to always give thanks to God for you, brothers loved by the Lord, because God chose you from the beginning for salvation through sanctification of the Spirit and belief in the truth; to which he called you through our Good News, for the obtaining of the glory of our Lord Jesus Christ.

2 Thessalonians 2:13-14

Somewhere between the wrong and the right,
Somewhere between the darkness and the light,
Somewhere between who I was and who you're making me,
Somewhere in the middle, you'll find me.
Somewhere in the Middle.
Casting Crowns[21]

I can assure you of two things about Discipleship Road. I know where it starts. It starts when you say yes to God, your moment of justifying grace, which reminds me of a saying from my dad, "He chased her and chased her until she turned around and caught him."

That's much the way it is with God and us. He chases and chases until we turn and catch him. That's the moment of justifying grace. The second thing I know is where Discipleship Road ends. It ends in the presence of God our Creator. Jesus has promised to come and lead us there (see Matthew 14:2-3).

What I can't tell you is how long the journey is, except to say it is a lifetime expedition. I have never met anyone who truly believed they had completed the Discipleship Road Course. Much like golf and tennis, there never comes a day where we have confidence that we have learned all we can learn and have gotten as good as we will ever be. There is always one more knot to untie, one more lesson to learn.

Now, maybe you're a driven achiever (I bear a strong resemblance here). If so, your natural reaction goes something like, "Why would I want to start something I can never complete?"

Such an undertaking would, on the surface, seem counter-productive. But what if the journey provided joy you couldn't find anywhere else? I wish I could compare it to something to help you get the sense of the joy and fulfillment that comes with this journey, but nothing even approaches it. For many others and for me, the effort is its own reward.

I am reminded of the profound observation from Jim Elliot, "He is no fool who gives what he cannot keep, to gain that which he cannot lose." Long before Jim Elliot, Jesus said it this way, "For whoever desires to save his life will lose it, but whoever will lose his life for my sake, the same will save it. For what does it profit a man if he gains the whole world, and loses or forfeits his own self?"

This walk up Discipleship Road will be the greatest adventure of your life and will provide endless memories. Yes, the going will be difficult at times, but that is the nature of life, irrespective of what route you choose, so choose the route that promises great victories and the life more abundant. Take this road that leads to the Father's house.

As I survey the road ahead of me and see the examples set by those who beckon me to follow, it seems the ones ahead of me are even more determined than I am to seek new insights to God. I am much more passionate, dedicated, and hungry for knowledge now than I was 10 years ago, and it in no way compares to where I was 20 years ago. This seems consistent with their experiences, as well.

The word that comes to mind here is perseverance. My life is one of perseverance, and I'll bet you see the same in yours. Now, when we think of perseverance, our minds generally turn to bearing through some difficulty, but that is not the only flavor of it. There is also the perseverance required to stick with something worthwhile and joyous, dedicating yourself to making it endure. My immediate thoughts in this realm come from my career. It has been a long and winding road with many peaks and valleys—and the peaks were much higher than the valleys were low. But I would rather share a love story—the story of perseverance that brought, and brings, me the most joy.

The story of perseverance in my marriage started when I was a freshman at Texas A&M. In a huge math class a friend of mine, Greg Knopp, said to me, "If you could date any girl in the room, which one would it be?"

Now, this was infinitely more interesting than the lecture, and pure fantasy. It was a really big room, and there were pretty girls everywhere I looked. But there was this one and, Oh my! It was as if a spotlight shone directly on her and all others faded to black and white. I told him, "The red haired girl towards the back, right there in the middle."

Now, you might be thinking about now how our strong Christian faiths drew us together in that moment, but it wouldn't be the truth. Her beauty defied description, and I was… well… an 18 year-old male. God and my faith walk did not enter into my considerations at the time at all. God, however, meant it for good, and I fell in love with her the first time I spoke to her. I loved her before she even knew I existed, a form of prevenient grace. Clearly, this was God's prevenient grace in action, the grace that goes before us.

I had to orchestrate an opportunity to "accidentally" run into her. I studied her comings and goings. So, having managed to run into her, I asked to borrow her notes from Biology—I had spotted her there as well. I knew if I got that notebook, I could find out her name, phone number, and where she lived. Not only did we not have Facebook then, Al Gore had yet to invent the Internet.

She was clearly out of my league, but I was committed to pursuing her anyway. I asked her out, and she said yes. This is where I tell you it was a particularly blissful evening, we fell madly in love, and everything proceeded from there. Actually, it was for me and I did fall in love. Not so much for her. There would be no second date.

I walked away but did not forget. Flash forward a year and I walk into a Business Law class and see her sitting there as beautiful as ever. My heart jumps and just for a minute I thought..., but then sensibility kicked in and I continued down about four rows (another huge lecture hall). And then she called my name, "Robert, come sit with me."

I could have bounded over those seats without touching the ground, but somehow I managed to muster all the cool I had and made it back up to where she sat. Imagine my utter disbelief when a couple of weeks later, she asked me on a date. We dated for three years, got married, and began a life together. This is where I tell you about "happily ever after."

Funny thing though, about that time, life happened. The "leaving your family and cleaving to one another" was our first challenge. Our parents weren't all that helpful there. Jobs and careers felt like a roller coaster at a Six Flags amusement park. Then two kids came along, two marvelous kids I can report now, but during the ride I would not always have given you that assessment. It hasn't been easy, but it has always been worthwhile.

But I never doubted my decision. Surely she did,

but I never did. Actually, I'm sure she did on a fairly regular basis. I'm not the easiest guy to live with, that's for sure, but I was committed to making it work, in spite of my failures.

Which brings me to my point. Stumbles and failures are inevitable, but that's when the perseverance kicks in. This story is as much about her grace and forgiveness as it is about my dedication to growing in our relationship. I can't even begin to count the times I have failed the relationship, failed her, failed as a father, or failed in some other fashion, at work, church and pretty much everywhere. Simple, mundane failures. Spectacular, tremendous failures.

It reminds me of a favorite hymn, "Stand by Me." The third verse contains these words, "In the midst of tribulation, stand by me. When I've done the best I can, and my friends misunderstand, Thou who knowest all about me, stand by me."[22] Even though she knows all about me, she stands by me anyway. Many times I didn't want to get up and start over, but she pushed me to persevere. She assured me, "We can do this."

This pattern of failure, forgiveness, and reconciliation takes me to the Bible. A Biblical scholar once told me he could cover the Bible in three easy steps so I would never forget it.

Step 1 - God created the heavens and the earth and it was good. That's Genesis 1 and 2.

Step 2 - Man made a mess of it. Genesis 3.

Step 3 - God has persisted and persevered in repairing the relationship ever since. You'll find that in Genesis 4 through Revelation 22.

Yes, it's an oversimplification, but it is accurate, and no, I haven't forgotten it.

This is the story of my marriage, my career, and my walk up Discipleship Road. I repeat, Discipleship Road is a long and winding road with many peaks and valleys. And the peaks are much higher than the valleys are low, but it is not a road you can successfully navigate on your own.

It's entirely possible you may be thinking right now that there comes a point where you have a solid enough foundation, are sufficiently accomplished in the five Disciple Disciplines and are blossoming in the fruit of the spirit to go it on your own. Such thoughts will lead you directly into a trap.

God said, *It is not good for the man to be alone.* (Genesis 2:18) It was true then, it remains so today. Man (which includes both men and women) was designed to be in relationship—with God, with a spouse, with family, and most certainly with friends and encouragers.

I have arrived at a place on Discipleship Road where I am deep, deep into study, almost all of it self-guided, and I find this is when I am at my most dangerous. It is so very easy to spin off course. I have watched it happen to friends and even some who were on my Spiritual Guides list. To avoid falling in the trap, I call on those ahead of me on Discipleship Road who know me to provide continuous assessment, correction, and redirection.

I recently made mention to one of them about Marcion, a follower of Jesus in the 2nd century. A pastor made some observations about Marcion that caused me to go back and study the man, and I found Marcion was introduced to Christ and became a devoted follower. He eventually divested himself of his highly successful shipping business and sailed to Rome where he contributed the sale proceeds (no small amount) to the church. There, he took up residence and poured himself into study.

Somewhere in his fervor, he took a wrong turn and concluded the world was not created by God, but by an evil demi-god. In his line of thinking, the true God did not come into existence until Jesus appeared on the earth to correct the mess created by the evil demi-god.

You can well imagine that the church was not enamored with his "revelation." I will also add that he had several other revolutionary ideas that were not at all compatible with Biblical teaching. You will not be surprised to learn he was summarily booted out of the church... but the story doesn't end there. He was so confident in his conclusions that he formed his own church, branches of which sprung up in several towns and cities and the movement lasted for almost 200 years, long after his death.

Why do I tell you this story? I tell you this story because it could well be my story absent my constant navigational check-ins with veteran Spiritual Guides. Over the years, I have had many epiphanies that revealed some novel hidden meaning in a Bible passage or story. With great enthusiasm, I rush to a Spiritual Guide (usually the one most handy at the moment) to share my magnificent revelation. Thankfully, I have been set straight each and every time. This is not to say I haven't had wonderful and valid Aha! moments, but I can tell you from experience it is oh so easy to get off track. I am confident I will never mature to a point where I don't have an ongoing, desperate need for Spiritual Guides until I leave this world.

Similarly, someone(s) in your path will always yearn for the guidance you can provide. Now you can view this as a chore that will never be done. (My dad always told me, "Do a job right the first time and you won't have to do it again." One bright day I responded, "Then why are you insisting I mow the grass again, because I did it right last week?" That was definitely the wrong response.) Or, you can see it for what it is: the greatest calling of your life.

A couple of years ago, I attended one of those leadership development courses and we were challenged to list the areas of our jobs from which we derived the highest sense of fulfillment. Once we had our list, we were told to dig deeper into each one looking for the elements that led to a sense of accomplishment.

As I worked through mine, I found that one of the sources of deepest satisfaction was in helping others succeed. I truly enjoy seeing others meet and exceed their goals. I find great joy in helping others in the workplace dig out of a jam.

This was not always the case. Actually, it was a bit of a revelation for me when working through the exercise. I remind you, I am the driven achiever. It has always been about my victories, my successes, often at the expense of others. I related earlier that I came to a point where I realized winning at the expense of others was not winning at all, but I had not noticed that somewhere along the way I became more interested in helping others succeed than in my own success.

You might well be shaking your head at such nonsense right now. All I can say is, I would have too ten years ago, too. The impact of walking Discipleship Road will amaze you.

I can't think of anything more worthwhile, anything more gratifying, than helping someone else down Discipleship Road... unless it is helping someone onto Discipleship Road. Further, there is absolutely no chance that God will stop putting people in your path along the way for you to help.

I opened this chapter by telling you this is a forever journey, and I know how terribly daunting that sounds. When I was a child, I was taught that heaven was a perfect place where I would live forever. When I reached a certain age, I asked what I would be doing forever and was told, "You'll do all your favorite things."

Well, when I got home I set about thinking that through. I asked myself what my favorite things were and the answers came back, "Playing football, riding my bike, and eating pizza." So, I sat there and thought more on it, and finally concluded that riding my bike endlessly coupled with a never-ending football game sounded like something I would grow tired of, and I frankly decided that being a Christian and following the example of Jesus was how I wanted to live, but I'll take a pass on this heaven thing, thank you very much.

Thankfully, I have a very different view of it now.

And so it is with discipleship. Once I committed to discipleship, I knew I needed the help of mentors and guides. By instinct I knew I needed people to coach me along the way. I didn't realize at the time how much encouragement it would require, though. What truly didn't register was that I would be called on to disciple others. Even when I grasped it was my responsibility to disciple others, I could never have imagined how joyful it could be.

This process of growing in Christian maturity is filled with surprises and new joys. On the surface, studying God and Jesus sounds like going back to school, and the prospect of never completing the course sounds like drudgery, as did going to heaven to the much younger me. But in ways you can't envision until you experience them, these acts of discipling are a never-ending source of excitement and joy. Leading others up Discipleship Road and sharing the experiences will surely provide the source of your greatest joys.

Let's go back to Genesis 2:18 where God declares, *It is not good for the man to be alone.* This moment introduces human relationships. Adam, who previously lived in solitude, now had to adjust to living in relationship with Eve. Eventually, they had Cain, Abel, and Seth and the concept of living as a family was instituted. And not long thereafter, those relationships grew into community life, which became an integral foundation of existence.

Next, hop with me to the New Testament. In Matthew 3, John baptizes Jesus. In Matthew 4, Jesus heads into the wilderness and, upon emerging from the wilderness, learns John has been arrested. Jesus decides to move his base of operations to Capernaum and immediately begins calling disciples. Here's the sequence: Jesus is baptized and initiates his ministry, Jesus wanders the wilderness and is tested by Satan, then Jesus emerges from the wilderness and builds a community of disciples.

We are designed to live in community and to nurture one another. Each of us develops a community, and yours is constantly changing. At any given time, several people will disciple you, and even more will appear over the course of your lifetime. Some people (not all) who disciple you today will fade out of your life, only to be replaced by others. This is natural. God sends the ones you need just as you need them.

Similarly, some of those you disciple will move away or out of your sphere of influence. This too is as it should be. I'm thinking of two specific relationships where I was discipling someone along the way, when they got really serious about this following Jesus thing and wholly committed to the five Discipleship Disciplines. They rocketed right past me on Discipleship Road as if I stood still. I could well have resented their progress or I could take advantage of it. In those cases where I realized what had happened, I elected to take advantage of it. I went from being the discipler to being the disciplee, and my life has been greatly enriched as a result.

I also want you to be aware there will be ebbs and flows in your pursuit of spiritual discipline. As the teacher said in Ecclesiastes, *There is a time for everything.*

You will find times in your life when you continue down the road in fellowship with your Spiritual Guides, not requiring much guidance or correction. At other times you will be desperate for intense counseling and direction. Times when the needs of others for your guiding hand will come like a flood as you attend to their needs. In other seasons, your time and attention will be better utilized elsewhere.

In the ebbs and in the flows, embrace the importance of the need for discipling, and never turn your back on its importance in your life.

Constant.
The word here is constant.
Constant awareness.
Constant growth and improvement.
Constant dedication and commitment.

Forever is... well... forever.

I now direct our attention to this wonderful world of growing in discipleship.

I reiterate – Disciple is a verb.

STUDY QUESTIONS

Do you find the prospect of embarking on Discipleship Road as daunting or terribly exciting?

We typically talk of perseverance in the context of bearing through a difficulty. Can you relate a time when you persevered in the context of something joyful?

Robert talked about the cycle of failure, forgiveness, and reconciliation. Is this a cycle that needs to be broken, or is it by its very nature a critical component of our spiritual growth?

Think back over your recent history. Identify times when you took a wrong turn that could have been avoided had you sought the guidance of others. Is there a pattern to these occurrences? If so, name it and by that I mean give it a direct label. This will help you see it coming when it approaches again.

CHAPTER 9

Growing in Discipleship

As newborn babies, long for the pure milk of the Word, that with it you may grow, if indeed you have tasted that the Lord is gracious: coming to him, a living stone, rejected indeed by men, but chosen by God, precious. You also, as living stones, are built up as a spiritual house, to be a holy priesthood, to offer up spiritual sacrifices, acceptable to God through Jesus Christ.

1 Peter 2:2-5

I love the journey of life. And when all is finished, I would like to be remembered, not as a teacher or as a scholar or even as a husband or father, as important as all of these are to me, but rather as a disciple of the Master, Jesus Christ. To be remembered as a disciple of Jesus means that people remember me for living life to the full as I follow Jesus into every area of life into which he leads me.

Michael J. Wilkins

Discipleship Road presents the greatest of all human journeys, and it is indeed an adventure. We often envision it as something to be achieved, a destination. I've written for eight chapters now about Discipleship Road. There is no road to Discipleship. Discipleship is the road.

When I set my eyes on a destination, I put my head down and zero in on the destination. I am one of those fathers who, once the car was packed, the family buckled in, the gas tank full, and the destination set, we weren't stopping for anything along the way until we had to gas up again. "Everyone out, go to the bathroom! I'm not stopping again, and no, you can't have a 44 oz. frozen soda! I just told you, I'm not stopping again!" This describes a trip, not an adventure.

Adventures, by contrast, are savored. Adventures are unpredictable. We engage in them as they unfold before us. We slow down and engage with those we encounter along the way. When confronted with something new, we stop and take it in rather than racing around it in order to be on our way.

God is calling you to join him on this great adventure and to join with others as we make this amazing journey up Discipleship Road. In the United Methodist ordination service, candidates are asked, "Are you going on to perfection?"

I was amazed at the audacity of such a question and was troubled that these brave men and women, literally kneeling before God, would answer "yes." And then a wizened pastor enlightened me by clarifying the question. The question is not, "Are you going to be perfect?" Rather it is, "Are you going on to perfection?" The immediately following question is, "Do you expect to be made perfect in this lifetime?" to which the candidates respond, "with God's help."

A double meaning lies within these inquiries. First, are you living a life that is becoming more Christ-like, more perfect? Second, are you living a life that leads to the Father's house where he will heal and perfect you? Now, those are questions to which I surely hope you can answer, "Yes!"

I stumble and fall, but I remain on the road to perfection. When I fall, Jesus picks me up and I amble on ahead, and it is not me or my actions that will perfect me. It is God and God alone who will do the perfecting. He does the same for all of his children who are willing to make the journey.

My mind wanders to that great scene in the gospels where Peter boldly asks Jesus to call him out onto the water, and Peter has the audacity to step out of the boat in faith when Jesus honors his request. It's not long, however, before Peter's attention is distracted by the waves and he sinks into the water. Watch what happens next. *Immediately Jesus stretched out his hand [and] took hold of him.* But don't stop there, read on.

This is one of those stories where the story jumps from one place to the next with no intervening explanation. I love those instances, because it forces me to think even deeper.

Look what happens next in Matthew's gospel. *Immediately Jesus stretched out his hand [and] took hold of him. When they got up into the boat, the wind ceased.*

How did they get back to the boat? One minute, Jesus plucked Peter out of the water and the next they climbed back into the boat. It's possible Jesus hurled Peter into the boat after Jesus caught him. Jesus might have blinked twice, like a scene out of *I Dream of Jeannie*, thereby transporting them magically into the boat. Or maybe it was a *Star Trek* moment, "Beam us back in the boat, Scotty."

I certainly don't envision Peter and the Lord dog-paddling back to the boat. In short, I just can't bring myself to embrace any of these options. Rather, I see Jesus arm-in-arm with Peter, walking back across the water as Jesus gently explains what Peter has just experienced.

This is what I experience when I stumble on the road to perfection.

Jesus sometimes accomplishes this catching and assuring through direct means, but most of the time he does it through others. He dispatches them to pick me up, assure me, and send me on my way. Ecclesiastes 4:9-10, *Two are better than one, because they have a good reward for their labor. For if they fall, the one will lift up his fellow; but woe to him who is alone when he falls, and doesn't have another to lift him up.*

That's Discipleship!

The destination is Jesus and my eyes are on him, to be more Christ-like each day, and Discipleship Road is the adventure that leads me there.

Growing!

Discipleship is not stagnant. It is action-packed. As we have explored, it is about cultivating the faith that has been planted in you. The step that naturally follows is planting that faith in others and nurturing it in them. This 'passing it on' is not secondary in importance, but only secondary in sequence. You can't plant and nurture in others what doesn't also grow in you.

And like any farmer or gardener will tell you, cultivation is an ongoing, never-ending process. You have to prepare the soil, plant the seeds, water, fertilize, weed, prune, and sometimes cross-pollinate. "That garden ain't gonna tend itself!"

God called mankind into partnership in this great institution we call Life on Earth. It started at the very beginning in the Garden of Eden, when Adam was charged with tilling and keeping the garden. He is still calling us to join him today. Do you not believe God could have cultivated the Garden of Eden all by his lonesome, or better yet, have created it where it was maintenance free? Of course he could, but he created humans for the purpose of having someone to be in relationship with him.

Fast-forward and we find Jesus commissioning his disciples to go into the world and make disciples. Do you not believe Jesus could have turned the entire world into disciples with a sweep of his hand? Of course he could. Nary a doubt in my mind, but his design was to create a partnership with mankind to engage in this divine work, in partnership with the likes of you and me, and the partnership continues today.

The wonderful evangelist, Tony Campolo, illustrates this so well. He tells of his youth and being awakened early each and every Saturday morning to help his dad wash the car. He hated being dragged out of bed, especially for such a routine and mundane task as washing the car. It wasn't until years later that he realized that his dad didn't need any help at all washing that car. It didn't even need washing on most Saturdays. No, his dad just wanted to spend time with him and to engage in a project together. And so it is with God and this earthly adventure—his creation hand-in-hand with his created.

Let's jump back on this road to perfection for a minute. I remind you once again what we covered in the last chapter: it is a journey of a lifetime. Done right, you will never complete it. This is truly the road that goes on forever.

At the risk of trivializing this adventure (and I surely don't want to leave that impression), it reminds me of video games I used to play. Not to say the road to perfection mimics a video game, but more that these video games mimic my journey on Discipleship Road.

I won't share the titles of games I played for fear of truly dating myself, but suffice it to say I played what has now evolved into Role Playing Games (RPG). In RPG, you are dropped into a time and place and you have to figure out where you are and how to navigate. You have at least some vague concept of the goal to be achieved, and along the way, you have to use your intellect, cunning, and the tools and skills you acquire to solve puzzles and conquer foes. You meet interesting characters and have to discern which are there to help and which are there to deter or confound you. Some are even intent on killing you. The farther you go in the game, the more challenging the puzzles and foes become.

In RPG you make friends and collect skills, tools, and weapons in order to solve the puzzles and conquer the foes. What I failed to add was that in most of these games there is some health-restoring mechanism: medical supply packs or magic potions. Early in my gaming experiences, I took great joy in finding these health-restorers as rewards for my accomplishments. I was well into gaming before I realized that, while the health-restoring mechanisms were critical to my success, the appearance of them along the path was a sign of an impending battle... and the more medi-packs that appeared, the bigger and more dangerous the foe around the next corner would be.

But that is not where I want to focus here. In playing the games, you get absorbed into the current objective—finding all the treasures, gathering the tools and weapons, obtaining new skills, and collecting the health-restoring devices, all the while imagining the foe at the end of the stage. Then suddenly the foe appears and there is no doubt this is THE

Foe, unlike the other minor challenges you have encountered.

Employing all your gathered skills and resources, you engage the beast. You are challenged like never before in the game. And then fight, fight, fight, and... Victory! The foe is defeated, the dragon is slain. A moment of great euphoria sweeps over you...

And then a door swings open, or a drawbridge opens, or a secret panel slides aside, and a new section of the game opens to a whole new territory. And this territory is brighter and grander than the one you just conquered, and you know—you just know—that new challenges await, and at the end of the new zone there will be yet another foe to challenge and defeat. Without a doubt, one more intimidating than the last.

On you go into the new world. Confident but wary, knowing you will get knocked down and knowing you will be tested.

This is the parallel I see to the greatest adventure of all: traveling Discipleship Road. Skills and treasures come our way as we develop the five Discipleship Disciplines. Spiritual Guides (and Worldly Guides) arrive to assist us on the journey, and our greatest victories tend to follow our most intimidating challenges. And every time we have a breakthrough or achieve a great victory, euphoria ensues and then new worlds and new opportunities open before us. At those junctures, we have the choice of sitting and reveling in our achievement or we can set about exploring the new vistas before us, knowing we will get knocked down in persevering towards the next victory.

As in RPG, we don't know how many chapters lie ahead, but we are eager to advance on the road to perfection. Yet another distinction, though, is that on the Road to Discipleship, the final victory is not ours, but God's.

Additional growth comes through discipling others. As you teach and lead them, you flush out weaknesses in your own knowledge and in your faith. It provides water and fertilizer for growing your faith and discipleship, and is not to be taken lightly.

Years ago when I worked for a very large public accounting firm, one of my duties was to lead training sessions for other staff members. While I thoroughly enjoyed my accounting duties, it was in leading training sessions that I found the most enjoyment. It was also where I discovered my deepest weaknesses in the subject matter I was charged with presenting. I never went into one of those sessions without adequate preparation providing me confidence I had mastery over the material. I never left one of those sessions confident I had command of the subject matter after all.

It was only through getting up and explaining the material that I began to see the cracks in my own understanding. Once I got through the material, the questions started coming from the students. "What about this?" and "What if this occurs?" "I had a situation where . . . what do you do then?"

I always left those sessions much less confident in my mastery of the subject, knowing there was much more to learn and I had better get to it, but also knowing I had learned a lot from the exchange with my students.

So, it is with discipleship. As you disciple others, questions will arise—questions they raise and more often questions you have of your own. It is your responsibility to set out on a quest to resolve those uncertainties. Sometimes through study, sometimes through prayer, more often through discussion with whomever is discipling you. These are the means by which we grow in discipleship.

Surely you've heard of the Circle of Life. This then is the Circle of Discipleship. I disciple you and you challenge me. For guidance I seek out those who disciple me and I grow in my discipleship. Then I return to you with increased knowledge and faith as we advance up Discipleship Road together.

Whom will you meet along the way?

There is no end to the variety of people you will meet along Discipleship Road. Many will be pilgrims on the road just like you. Others are there to provide counsel and guidance. Some come alongside to encourage you. Some will lead you astray, often the very ones you first see as guides or encouragers.

A significant segment of the epistles is devoted to imploring us to be wary of false teachers, those who will lead us off the path. I have come to be particularly wary of those who come saying they have all the answers. A pastor friend of mine suggested a book entitled *If You Meet the Buddha on the Road, Kill Him!*[23] by Sheldon Kopp, required reading for all seminary students in his day. I chased it down and found the major premise of the book to be if someone professes they have found "the Buddha" (the answer), you should kill the Buddha for it is surely a false Buddha. No one has all the answers, let alone the answer that solves all of life's mysteries.

In other words, there is no Buddha. Even equipped with the Holy Bible and guided by the Holy Spirit, no one has resolved all the mysteries of the faith. Hence, Paul's command in Philippians 2:12 to *work out your own salvation with fear and trembling.*

I have found this to be a most useful outlook in so many areas of my life. In all complicated matters, there is rarely a single right answer that makes all challenges fade away. I caution you to be wary of folks who will tell you they have the answer or who tell you "If only you will X. . . life will be blissful."

Life is a great wrestling match. Like Jacob on the banks of the River Jabbok, each of us is to wrestle with the scriptures and God's purpose for our lives.

God created each of us in a unique way because we each have a different role to play in the bringing of his kingdom. While we have commonalities and similarities, we do not all have the same callings on our lives. What brings great joy to you may be of minor significance to me. The things that will encourage me to fulfill the purpose for which I was designed may be of relative unimportance to you because you are here to fulfill something completely different. What comes easy for you may be entirely beyond my capabilities and vice versa.

While there are some immutable truths (e.g., there is a God, I am not he, he created this world, Jesus is the Son of God and Redeemer of the world), there is rarely a single right answer to the challenges we face in daily living; therefore, I am increasingly wary of those who claim to have "the answer."

I am equally distrustful of those who will dismiss their walk with God as being no big deal, and equally of those who make it too big a deal. Years ago, I played a lot of slo-pitch softball, I mean a lot of slo-pitch softball. From time to time, I would put together a team to play in a weekend tournament or I needed a replacement player for one of our standing teams. I would start by asking around. My standard question was, "Do you play?"

Quite often the response would be, "Oh yeah, I've been on fifteen All-Star teams and been MVP on six of them. We won State in 19xx." Rarely did these players ever live up to their self-billings.

Another common response went something like, "Oh, not really. I kinda play for fun on a team or two." Interestingly enough, these self-assessments generally turned out to be pretty accurate.

My favorite response though was, "Oh, I play a little." These were the players most team managers would pass on by, but not I. Rather than accept this answer at face value, I learned to probe a little. I came to learn that these were more often than not just the players I was after. "Playing a little" was a euphemism for "I really love the game and play really hard, but I'm never as good as I would like to be." Those were the guys I came to treasure.

And so it has been for me with teachers and mentors. Sure, the N. T. Wrights and Marcus Borgs and Charles Swindolls of the world have reputations that precede them. No one is going to buy "Oh, I write a little" or "Oh, I teach a little" from them.

But those luminaries aside, I am increasingly attracted to the humble teacher/mentor servants whose attitudes are, "Oh, I enjoy working with others on their discipleship, but I have so far to go with my own." These are the men and women at whose feet I want to sit and learn.

My advice to you is this: Kill the Buddhas, sit at the feet of the sages, and engage with everyone in between. Each has something to offer worth learning and most are eager to share what they have with you.

Whom shall I follow?

Let's go back to our definition of a disciple. A disciple is a learner, an apprentice. And all apprentices have to have a teacher, or, in my case many, many teachers.

Armed with what we have now covered about

discipleship, I send you back to the list of people you follow, the list you refined in Chapter 4. I trust you can now view that list with a new perspective. Go back and re-sort the list, knowing what you now know.

This is the best exercise I know for discerning whom you should follow. It will also serve as a reminder that you need to periodically review and update the list. New people will come onto your path. Over time you will find your needs, as well as the needs of others around you, will change and you'll have to adjust accordingly.

Where are the boundaries?

Boundaries? What boundaries? There are no boundaries.

Your discipleship must be all-encompassing. It must penetrate every aspect of your life. Even if your life is compartmentalized in great detail (career over here; family over there; hobby in a little nook down there; sports around the corner, etc.), there is no compartment where your discipleship should not reside.

Your discipleship must be intentional. Don't forget for a minute that your discipleship must be intentional. You must work at it every day and seek new ways to grow and in bringing others along with their faith. It can't be a "when I get around to it" endeavor. You have to seek it out.

Your discipleship must be consistent. You have to carry your discipleship with you in all aspects of your life at all times. You can't be expounding the gospels one minute and degrading co-workers the next. Integrity is about being consistent and doing as you say. Discipleship calls for integrity.

Your discipleship must be constant. You can't turn it on and off during the day. You can't decide to commit it to it today and leave it behind tomorrow. You can't take a week off. "Growing my discipleship is really hard, I need a break, and I'm on vacation for the next week so it's a good time for a break from discipleship, too."

Growing in discipleship is either integral to whom you are, or you're just playing around with it. Playing around with it will not advance your journey on Discipleship Road.

Return to Zechariah

Thus says the Lord of hosts: "Yahweh of Armies says: *In those days, ten men will take hold, out of all the languages of the nations, they will take hold of the skirt of him who is a Jew, saying, 'We will go with you, for we have heard that God is with you.'* Zechariah 8:23

Discipling is a path that will invite others to seek you out. They will see qualities in your character they want for themselves. They will want to attach to your robe so they may have what you have. The ancient Jews had a saying, "May you walk so closely with your rabbi that you are covered in his dust." People should want to be covered by your dust.

Look at the hem of your robe from time to time to see who has attached there. Reach out to them; make yourself available; find what they seek from you and give it to them. There is a line in Casting Crowns song "Does Anybody Hear Her?" that says, "With all the lost and lonely people searching for the hope that's tucked away in you and me."[24] Don't deprive them of the hope they seek that is indeed tucked away in you.

Then look around for those who should benefit by your discipling who aren't reaching for the hem of your robe. Take the time to engage with them and begin the exploration of what it is they seek in their lives. Look inside yourself and discover what you have to offer and how you can help move them along Discipleship Road.

And while you're looking down and around, look to see who is reaching out to disciple you. Assess whether they lead where you want to go and, if you do indeed see merit in their direction, engage with them. Cover yourself in their dust.

And finally, look up. God is ever seeking your attention. God wants your eyes cast in his direction. After all, it is God that is intentionally, consistently, constantly putting these people in your path on Discipleship Road so that you may move on to perfection, taking as many people along with you as possible.

Disciple is a verb!
.

STUDY QUESTIONS

Are you going on to perfection? Is this a goal you can embrace?

Reflect on times in the past when you stumbled and Jesus picked you up. Now that you have identified times when he saw you through in spite of your mistakes, do you doubt he'll carry you into the future? Why would he bring you this far only to abandon you now?

Robert says, "You can't plant and nurture in others what doesn't also grow in you." Do you agree? Is it possible to plant and nurture in others what doesn't grow in you?

Do you believe God could right all the wrongs in his creation? Why does he invite us to partner with him in this work if he could easily fix it on his own?

Name a time when God placed resources in your path (people, tools, healing methods, money) ahead of you just when you were going to need them.

Do you believe there is a single answer to life's challenges or are you wary of those who claim to have "the answer?"

Are you prepared to embark on this discipleship journey, an all-encompassing journey without borders?

Epilogue

God said, "Let the earth yield grass, herbs yielding seeds, and fruit trees bearing fruit after their kind, with their seeds in it, on the earth"; and it was so. The earth yielded grass, herbs yielding seed after their kind, and trees bearing fruit, with their seeds in it, after their kind; and God saw that it was good. There was evening and there was morning, a third day.

Zechariah 8:23

"He is no fool who gives what he cannot keep, to gain that which he cannot lose."

Jim Elliot

What is our purpose? Why are we here? What is our mission?

Man has struggled with these questions well before the written word, and while many answers have been offered, all fall short.

Here's what I believe, though. We are here to grow in love for Jesus Christ, Son of God, to grow in his likeness, to return to our true nature, and to live in the presence of God. While that sounds like multiple answers, it really is a single unit. God's original plan was to live in intimate relationship with his magnum opus: Man.

In Genesis 3, it says God was walking in the garden in the cool of the day, and I have the overwhelming sense that this was the highlight of his daily routine. Ever since Adam and Eve broke the relationship with God, he has longed to repair it and he sent Jesus to broker this reconciliation. Jesus was very clear that he is the way back to the father, so it stands to reason, as we seek Christ-likeness, we are moving toward all of the above. We follow Jesus engaging others in groups, large and small, and by inviting others on this journey to become disciples of Christ.

Discipling is active.

Discipling is intentional.

Discipling takes effort.

Yes – disciple is a verb.

In the beginning, God created the heavens and the earth. And on the third day, Genesis tells us, *God said, 'Let the earth yield grass, herbs yielding seeds, and fruit trees bearing fruit after their kind, with their seeds in it, on the earth'; and it was so. The earth yielded grass, herbs yielding seed after their kind, and trees bearing fruit, with their seeds in it, after their kind; and God saw that it was good.*

This creation story is one we have heard over and over, yet even here there are tiny details that we tend to pass over, little seeds of wisdom.

It says God created *herbs yielding seeds* and *fruit with seed in it* and fruit *with their seeds in it after their kind*. Seeds, actual seeds.

Whenever I read this passage previously, my focus was on the vegetation, to the extent I focused on the passage at all. I was always too eager to get on to the animals and the greatest of his creations – me: I mean mankind. But when I slow down, I can't help but notice the seeds. Seeds are mentioned three times in this passage. To be mentioned three times, there must be something significant here… and there is.

What the author tells us is God created a self-perpetuating world. All flora and fauna on this earth are designed to be self-propagating. The trees bear fruit that contain the seeds that will in turn become the next generation of trees. The animals bear the "seed" that will germinate the next generation of their species.

Reading on, we find that as the waters recede from the Great Flood, God instructs Noah, *Go out of the ship, you, and your wife, and your sons, and your sons' wives with you. Bring out with you every living thing that is with you of all flesh, including birds, livestock, and every creeping thing that creeps on the earth, that they may breed abundantly in the earth, and be fruitful, and multiply on the earth.*

Multiply and be fruitful. Fruitful. Contemplate that word—fruitful—and you find yourself back in the Garden with the *trees bearing fruit with seed in it.*

And then the oft-quoted mandate to Noah and his sons just before God creates his covenant with Noah, *Be fruitful and increase in number and fill the earth.* Noah and his sons are to go and propagate our species. There is seed in mankind whereby the next generation will be generated.

Even more famously, God makes covenant with Abraham, inspiring Abraham with these words,

Look now toward the sky, and count the stars, if you are able to count them, and continues, *So shall your offspring be,* or seed in many translations. The Jewish faith is grounded right here in these promises, and it is on this Judaic foundation that the whole of Christianity is built.

Seeds. Life giving seeds. Life sustaining seeds. Life perpetuating seeds.

Why then would it be any different with perpetuating the faith?

Jesus used many agricultural images to communicate with his disciples and followers. He planted the seeds of faith in his disciples, and created the New Covenant through them. He assured Thomas, *Because you have seen me, you have believed; blessed are those who have not seen and yet have believed.* As he was leaving them, his parting words included the following command, *Therefore go and make disciples of all nations.*

Jesus implored his disciples to nurture the seeds of faith he planted in them and to go and do likewise—to go and plant seeds of faith in others. We call that discipleship.

Thankfully, they took up his challenge. Not at first, but once he appeared to them, they got to it.

Post-Pentecost, the disciples fanned out and boldly proclaimed Jesus. They scattered the seeds of the faith far and wide. We have evidence of Thomas (no doubter, he) founding churches as far away as India. Paul planted seeds in Silas and Timothy, who in turn scattered the seeds of faith into the next generation.

This repetition of germinating the faith continues into this day, and it has been said it only takes one generation to neglect this duty for the light to go out completely.

We are the next generations of disciples. We are being called to propagate the faith, and our responsibility comes in two parts: nurture the seeds planted in us and plant seeds in others.

This is our calling in life.

This is our purpose.

To plant and cultivate.

Go and do likewise.

Disciple is indeed a verb.

NOTES

1 - Music by Singh and Lyrics by anonymous circa 1860
2 - Sanders 2007, 27
3 - Casting Crowns 2003
4 - Bugbee, Cousins and Hybels 199
5 - Acuff 2015, 93
6 - Augsburger 2006, 29
7 - Buchanan 2003, 252
8 - Watson 1998, 8
9 - Watson 1982, 49-50
10 - Iverson 1982
11 - Sammis 1964, 223
12 - Lucado 1989, dust jacket
13 - Buechner 1973, 14
14 - Augsburger 2006, 95
15 - MacArthur 1991, 17
16 - Blanchard and Johnson 2003
17 - McGrath 2010, 66
18 - Ivory 2008, 5
19 - Lucado 1985, xvi
20 - Main 2003, 40
21 - Casting Crowns 2007
22 - Tindley 1964, 544
23 - Kopp 1972
24 - Casting Crowns 2005

BIBLIOGRAPHY

Acuff, J. (2015). *Do Over: Rescue Monday, Reinvent Your Work, and Never Get Stuck*. New York, NY: Portfolio Penguin Group.

Augsburger, D. (2006). *Dissident Discipleship A Spirituality of Self-Surrender, Love of God, and Love of Neighbor*. Grand Rapids, MI: Brazos Press.

Blanchard, K., & Johnson, S. (2003). *The One Minute Manager*. William Morrow.

Buchanan, M. (2003). *The Holy Wild, Trusting in the Character of God*. Grand Rapids, MI: Ann Spangler and Associates.

Buechner, F. (1973). *Wishful Thinking : A Theological ABC*. New York: Harper & Row Publishers.

Bugbee, B. L., Cousins, D., & Hybels, B. (1994). *Network The Right People...In the Right Places...For the Right Reasons*. Grand Rapids, MI: Zondervan Publishing.

Hall, M., & Chapman, S. C. (Composers). (2003). The Voice of Truth. [Casting Crowns, Performer] On *Casting Crowns* [LP]. Beach Street Records.

Hall, M. (Composer). (2005). Does Anybody Hear Her. [Casting Crowns, Performer] On *Lifesong* [LP]. Beach Street Records.

Hall, M. (Composer). (2007). Somewhere in the Middle. [Casting Crowns, Performer] On *The Altar and the Door*. Beach Street Records.

Iverson, D. (Composer). (1982). Spirit of the Living God. Carol Stream, IL: Hope Publishing Company.

Ivory, L. (2008). *The Rhythm of Discipleship*. Geneva Press.

Kopp, S. B. (1972). *If You Meet a Buddha in the Road, Kill Him! The Pilgrimage of Psychotherapy Patients*. Palo Alto, CA: Science & Behavior Books Publishers.

Lucado, M. (1985). *On the Anvil, Stories on Being Shaped Into God's Image*. Wheaton, IL: Tyndale House Publishers, Inc.

Lucado, M. (1989). *Six Hours One Friday: Anchoring to the Power of the Cross*. Sisters, OR: Multnohma Books.

MacArthur, J. (1991). *Making Disciples*. Chicago, IL: Moody Press.

Main, B. (2003). *If Jesus Were a Senior, Last Minute Preparations for a Post-collegiate Life*. Louisville, KY: Westminster John Knox Press.

McGrath, A. (2010). *Mere Theology: Christian Faith and the Discipleship of the Mind*. London: SPCK.

Music by Singh, S. S., & Lyrics by anonymous. (circa 1860). "I Have Decided to Follow Jesus".

Sammis, J. H. (1964). When We Walk With the Lord. *The Book of Hymns*. The United Methodist Publishing House.

Sanders, J. O. (2007). Spiritual Discipleship. Chicago, IL: Moody Publishers.

Tindley, C. A. (Composer). (1964). When the Storms of Life are Raging. On *The Book of Hymns*. The United Methodist Publishing House.

Watson, D. L. (1982). *Called and Committed, World Changing Discipleship*. Wheaton, IL: H. Shaw Publishers.

Watson, D. L. (1998). *Covenant Discipleship, Christian Formation through Mutual Accountability*. Eugene, OR: Wipf and Stock Publishers

ACKNOWLEDGEMENTS

First, to God who years ago opened a door and dared me to walk through it, saying, "Robert write a book." Fortunately for him, Moses and Abram didn't drag their feet as long as I did.

Next, to Jim who is not only the engine that drives my writing, but he also serves as Chief Encourager. Each week, he takes my thoughts and reflections and magically weaves them into the works that appear as McBurnett's Musings. He constantly urged me on when the going got tough in driving this book to completion.

I am especially indebted to Bill, Jim, John, Steve, and Tom who bore through multiple drafts of the manuscript for this book. Your insights and recommendations shine through in the finished product.

Thanks to Lance and Drew who arrived in God's timing with encouragement and support that elevated the book beyond what it would have been absent their assistance. You truly created opportunities that wouldn't have existed otherwise.

I owe an unpayable debt to those who have discipled me on Discipleship Road, those whose examples appear in the book and tens of dozens of others, too. God is constantly sending people my way to keep me on the path often in subtle roles, other times in incredibly obvious roles. I thank you all.

I have been incredibly blessed by a long line of pastors, extraordinary shepherds. More than spiritual guides, friends. God has a calling for each person he created, but those he calls into ordained service are a breed apart. Thank you for saying yes to his invitation.

God designed us for us for relationship and he has placed me in incredible communities – Bible studies, Sunday school classes, Walk teams serving the Walk to Emmaus, business teams at work, sports teams and countless others. I thank each of you for tolerating my constant AHA Moments and setting me straight all those times when, like Peter, I rushed in with an impulsive, yet incorrect answer. Thanks for your always gentle, direct and often swift rebukes.

To Cynthia Stone at TREATY OAK PUBLISHERS, thank you for making an author out of me. I came to you a writer, and you turned me into an author. You took a near-complete manuscript, sprinkled it with magic pixie dust, and made it dance. Thanks for your patience with my seemingly unending questions and doubts, and for the many blessings at your skillful hands. Masterful indeed.

And to my wife Christy who daily shows God's love and grace to me in small and immense ways. I am blessed to have you illuminating my walk with God, pushing me towards a deeper and intimate relationship with God. You are truly God's gift that lights my path.

About the Author

Robert McBurnett is an everyday kind of guy constantly striving to grow in discipleship of Jesus Christ, while reaching out to help others in pursuit of discipleship. Robert's executive career in finance and accounting wound through senior leadership positions with a Major League Baseball club, a National Football team, a large metropolitan church and a charter school system, all the while accompanied by Jesus Christ every step of the way.

A man of great Biblical understanding, Robert has come to see God's hand in his daily activities. He invites you to share in his insights, questions, and personal experiences. As a disciple of Jesus Christ, Robert asks the questions that make us all think and allow us to grow closer in our own Christian walk.

Robert's previous book is *Exploring Life in the Context of Scripture*, a collection of thoughts and reflections that appeared in his weekly blog McBurnett's Musings.

Join him at
mcburnettsmusings.wordpress.com
and
rcmcburnett@gmail.com.